MAKE 'EM R...

A comedian's handbook

Volume One

MICHAEL KILGARRIFF

SAMUEL FRENCH

NE... ...YWOOD

ublishing Ltd
iael Kilgarriff, 1973
© Wolfe Publishing, 1973

Revised and re-written in 1979
© 1979 Michael Kilgarriff

The Pigtail of Li Fang Fu © 1919 by Reynolds Music
The Miner's Dream of Home © 1891 by Francis Day & Hunter Ltd
We All Come Into the World With Nothing © 1907 by B. Feldman & Co Ltd
Twelve Minute Old Time Act © 1979 Michael Kilgarriff

The material in this book may be used without payment of a fee

ISBN 0 573 19004 6

Samuel French Ltd
26 Southampton Street   Strand   London WC2 7JE

MADE AND PRINTED IN GREAT BRITAIN BY
LATIMER TREND & COMPANY LTD PLYMOUTH

MADE IN ENGLAND

CONTENTS

ACKNOWLEDGEMENTS

Material from *The Pigtail of Li Fang Fu* is reproduced by permission of Reynolds Music. The full and original text of the monologue is published, with music, by Reynolds, who will supply a catalogue and price list of their full range of monologues on request. Their address is: Reynold's Music, EMI Music Publishing Ltd, Distribution Centre, 64 Dean Street, London W1V 6QD.

The song *The Miner's Dream of Home* is reproduced by permission of Francis, Day and Hunter, EMI Music Publishing Ltd, 138–40 Charing Cross Road, London, WC2H 0LD. The music can be obtained from this address.

The words of the song *We All Come into the World With Nothing* is reproduced by permission of Feldman's, EMI Music Publishing Ltd, Distribution Centre, 64 Dean Street, London W1V 6QD.

By the same author

IT GIVES ME GREAT PLEASURE (pub. Samuel French)
THE GOLDEN AGE OF MELODRAMA
COMIC SPEECHES FOR ALL OCCASIONS (pub. Futura)

Compilations
1,000 JOKES FOR CHILDREN (pub. Ward Lock)
BEST SHOW BIZ JOKES, ETC., ETC.

Sketches (pub. Samuel French)

THREE MELODRAMAS
THREE MORE MELODRAMAS
MUSIC HALL MISCELLANY

AUTHOR'S NOTE

As a result of what were to me incomprehensibly convoluted publishing difficulties my first comedian's handbook, *Make 'Em Laugh*, went out of print after the sell-out of the first edition in 1973.

Despite continued demand it remained virtually unobtainable until French's agreed to republish in two parts. A careful filleting and updating of my original text forms the bulk of this present volume, and as there have been so many alterations—I hope for the better—I decided upon a fresh title.

Should *Make 'Em Roar—Volume One* meet with your approval, therefore, the rest of the 1973 version plus more additional material will appear in due course.

My grateful thanks are due to my partner, Johnny Dennis, for his practical assistance and helpful comments, and to Noël Woolf of French's for his enthusiasm and encouragement.

MICHAEL KILGARRIFF
Ealing, February 1979

INTRODUCTION

One thing I ought to say at the outset is that I don't pretend for one moment that all the gags listed herein are either new or original—indeed few of them fall into either category. What I *do* say is that all of them are usable for the working comic, whether amateur or professional.

In any case, if a gag is a really good one, it will always stand telling again . . . and again . . . and again. For instance, in the autumn of 1969, I found myself with Brian Rix's "Theatre of Laughter" Company for *She's Done It Again!* by Michael Pertwee. At one stage in rehearsals a problem arose as to how the late Leo Franklyn should best make an exit. I duly suggested the chambermaid gag (22) which happened to fit the plot and the situation at that point. This is of course a very hoary old jest indeed, but my suggestion was accepted and became one of the biggest laughs in the show—in a run of seven months at the Garrick Theatre and fourteen weeks on tour it invariably elicited a delighted roar and a round of applause. Now, I don't believe that our audiences hadn't heard this joke before, but, like an old and valued friend, they were happy to greet it again.

Caution: I don't want to impose upon you the manner in which to tell a funny story. Six comedians may tell the same joke, they will all be different and they will all be funny. The actual words I have used in setting down the gags are intended merely to give the gist—when I tell them myself I probably tell them quite differently from the way I have written them, so you in turn should adapt the material to suit your own personality and style.

If you haven't found a style and are dubious about your personality—sing a song instead.

HOW TO TELL A FUNNY STORY
(and live with yourself afterwards)

Preparation

Like sex, the only way to do it is to do it. Unlike sex, however, you are expected to tell a funny story in public, which makes it different.

Of course, for me just to say "do it" isn't much help if you've never done it before, or if you haven't done very much of it. You can try out a comedy routine on your family, but this is dangerous since their reaction will be unreliable. In fact I don't recommend you to try out your routine on anybody but yourself. If you have confidence in your material, have practised your routine until you can get through it without a lot of "umming" and "er-ing", then just get on stage and belt out the gags without a seeming care in the world. If nobody laughs, you'll still get a good hand when you finish—they'll be glad to see you go.

Technique

It is exceedingly difficult to discuss technique in general terms, since the telling of funny stories is such a personal business. But the first thing I would advise is: don't go on too long. If you feel you're not going down well, get off; if you feel you're going over very big—get off just the same. I've so often seen a comic ruin a successful act by staying on for just that bit too long.

Make sure you tell the story logically and get to the meat of the gag quickly. A long, slow build-up is only justifiable if the gag is a gilt-edged, sure-fire smackeroo—and even then it is best to have a few "booster" gags along the way.

Speak rapidly, pausing at relevant places to let the story-line sink in. Repeat the odd line to make sure that the sense is reaching the back of the gallery, and then punch out the tag line clearly and distinctly, perhaps lifting the volume a decibel or two.

A Gag Analysed
As written:

"My mother-in-law! . . . what a man! When I told her I wanted to marry her daughter she said, 'How dare you! You marry my daughter? You're effeminate . . .!' *Me*, effeminate! Mind you, next to her I am . . ."

As told:

"My mother-in-law! My mother-in-law . . ."

(*Repeat "mother-in-law" and pause. The very words set up a conditioned reflex and will get a chuckle*)

"... what a man! ..."   (*Longish pause for the laugh. It takes a little time for this one to sink in*)

"When I told her I wanted to marry   (*This to be spoken rapidly*)
her daughter, she said, 'How dare   (*Spoken slower—it is important for
you! You—marry my daughter?   this part of the story-line to get across*)

You're effeminate!' "   (*Longish pause for the audience to work out what the word "effeminate" means and then to savour future possibilities*)

"Me—effeminate!"   (*Spoken in shocked tones, then pause*)

"Mind you—next to her, I *am*!"   (*Spoken rapidly and lifting the last two words*)

This may seem an overly academic and cold-blooded way of presenting a gag, but I have laid it out in detail to show the maximum effect to be gleaned from the simplest of jokes. In the routines in the pages to follow I have not attempted to analyse every joke as minutely as above—the result would be as tedious for you to read as for me to write—but I hope that these examples will encourage the neophyte to look at his material a little more carefully to see what can be extracted over and above the obvious tag-line reactions.

It is in the nature of club work that the comic will find his quickest response from the front of the audience, but don't ignore the poor folks at the back who will feel more and more alienated if the comic appears to be having a private party with his friends down at the front; where there is a circle give the people up there the benefit of your big blue eyes and flashing smile once in a while.

Any accents or dialects which you can do well (and only if you *can* do them well) should be incorporated into your stories. A tag-line is doubled in effect if delivered in the appropriate Burnley or Glasgow accent, besides giving you the chance to display yet another facet of your coruscating talents.

Jokes should be acted out. When telling a tale about something dreadful that happened to yourself or to a friend the impact is greatly heightened if the comic appears genuinely appalled or frightened or embarrassed as the case may be; the resultant climax will be all the funnier for the contrast—contrast and surprise being the essence of comedy, as all pundits agree.

Local references are always popular. I always spend a few minutes poring over a map of the area where I happen to be appearing to see which local street-names or districts can be capitalized upon. Notorious clubs and pubs can be pressed into service, as can local personalities such as famous sportsmen or Members of Parliament. Nor should national and international events be ignored: a General Election gives the comic a chance to have a tilt at politicians in general, which always goes down well.

British and American audiences have an endearing habit of applauding long stories, which is always encouraging and helps to fill up your allotted time—and it is worth remembering that long jokes are especially appreciated by audiences of old-age pensioners.

Long jokes are also useful for lending variety to an act, for giving a change of gear, and for providing your audience with a breather from all those hysterically funny one-liners and brief quips with which you started your act, and which you will intersperse between the lengthier stories. Incidentally, when I talk about long jokes I do not mean shaggy dog stories which have no place in a stage act. Rather do I mean stories like the budgie joke (number 160) or the cat joke (number 58), which can either be told straight through or spun out with plenty of booster gags.

Special Occasions

If you are performing for a special event you should take the trouble to make some references to the occasion in your routine. A firm's annual dinner will give you the chance to make a few remarks about the firm's lousy products and to put in a good word for a rival company; a golf club dance means the inclusion of golfing stories; at a charity fête the local secretary can be your Aunt Sally. That the work-force are underpaid and the management overpaid will always go down well: "I'd like to thank Stan the nightwatchman for making me a cup of tea, and I'd like to thank the Managing Director for drinking it for me," is the kind of artless gag which will always be received with roars of approval.

Risqué Stories

What is acceptable and what isn't in the content of a story depends on so many factors that I will not attempt to lay down any hard and fast rules. But I will say this: the law of diminishing returns applies to patter acts as to anything else, and there *are* subjects to joke about other than sex.

How far should you go? The venue, the town, the age and composition of your audience, even the time of day—all these must be taken into consideration. An act at a rugger club stag night would be disastrous if it were not as blue as the Danube; a charity affair at the village hall where you are introduced by the vicar would be even more disastrous if it were. You must use your own judgment and common sense about this question, and perhaps take advice from the manager or someone local who knows the tastes of the audience. If you have any qualms about a particular gag—cut it. It may be a stunningly good wheeze in your opinion, but if you offend and/or embarrass your audience you will have a very hard time winning them over again.

Sex may be a perfectly valid subject for humour, but as I have said before, there are other ways of being funny.

Starting a Joke

There isn't much to say on this point since nowadays microphones and deafening amplification ensure that the comic can be heard without his

having to exert himself to any degree. As Norman Vaughan said to me:
"When you've got that mike—you're the *guv'nor!*" The old-style technique
might still be found useful in a hall without mikes, however—this was
generally a come-hither scooping gesture of the hand accompanied by the
enjoinder: "Here . . . no, listen a minute . . ."

If you are topping a laugh on a previous joke it is often worthwhile to
repeat the first few words of a story. This ensures that there are no dead-
spots in the act and that the plot of the next joke is understood. For
instance:

"This chap walked into a pet shop . . .   (*As laugh from previous gag dies
                                                                             down*)
No, listen; this chap walked into a—   (*If one man is still laughing*)
Have you just worked it out?   (*Pause*)
Well, put it back. This chap walked—   (*Pause for big laugh*)
No, come on, we've got a lot to get
through, and I want to get home before
the pills wear off . . . so this chap
walked into a pet shop etc., etc."

If you are telling a story which includes a number of "he saids", be sure
it is clear who is saying what. Generally the sense of the story will make it
apparent, but a tip is to alter the direction in which you are facing, i.e. in
joke number 160 the man wanting to buy the budgie can be indicated by
facing slightly left and the man behind the counter by facing slightly right.

Timing

Timing is such a delicate and elusive art that I will not attempt any defini-
tion, instruction or advice. It is so totally instinctive—though it is also a
gift which can be improved with practice—that I firmly believe it cannot be
taught. Timing depends ultimately on your style. Ken Dodd is celebrated
for his zany quick-fire delivery just as Jack Benny was renowned for his
slow burn. Both techniques are valid; whether one or the other or something in between is right for you only you can decide.

Finishing a Joke

It is often said that a good comic never laughs at his own jokes. I would
say that this is only a very general precept; some comics—Charlie Williams,
Ken Goodwin, Norman Wisdom, Danny La Rue—make a point of breaking this rule to great effect, and of course Basil Brush's cackle is his trade-
mark. However, it is probably better on the whole to let your audience
laugh first. You can even look bewildered on a tag-line, such as:

"On my way here I met a Scotsman in   ("*On my way here*" *can be
a kilt—I could tell he was a genuine   changed to* "*in the High Street*"
Scot 'cos he had dandruff on his   *or any other local reference*)
boots. . . .

But the odd thing about this chap was that he was wearing his kilt upside down! . . . *(Pause for the picture to sink in)*

Upside down! . . . I said to him 'why are you wearing your kilt upside down?' He said, 'I'm going to a fancy-dress ball.' *(Pause)*
I said, 'What as?' He said, 'A shuttlecock!' " *(This said with speed, then look puzzled. As the laugh subsides you can say, "I'm still trying to work that out . . .")*

Once when I had told this gag a man shouted out, "Explain it!" This got a big laugh, to which I replied, "Certainly, sir—" I then did a big double-take at the back of the hall and said, "Oh, good evening, officer . . ." and carried on with the next gag.

While on the subject of repartee I would like to suggest that you have a stock of standard heckle-squashers in readiness (*"remind me to come to your parents' wedding!"*) if you feel your native wit is not up to dealing with interruptions on their own terms. But you should aim at answering hecklers in kind rather than just throwing out insults—the whole question of heckling is dealt with in my book *It Gives Me Great Pleasure* (Samuel French) and I shall not enlarge on it here since it is not in general a problem for the beginner.

Style

First of all you must decide whether you are going to present yourself as "straight" or eccentric—the cynic or the innocent. The straight comics are those who dress smartly and appear as dapper, trendy men-about-town; the eccentrics are clownish or grotesque in their appearance, using funny hats, make-up, props, and above all, funny faces.

But even the straight comic will develop his strongly individual style, such as Ted Rogers (hard, punchy, wise-cracking), Jimmy Tarbuck (lovable Liverpudlian scamp), Dave Allen (suave and sophisticated), Larry Grayson (limp-wristed and epicene); celebrated drolls of today include Ken Dodd (buck teeth, unruly hair, manic delivery), Harry Secombe (enormous girth and bubbling extravert personality), and Freddie Davies (lisp and rubber features).

Then there are the speciality comedians: Jimmy Edwards with his brass playing, Charlie Drake with his slapstick, Billy Dainty with his eccentric dancing, Rod Hull with his Emu, Max Wall with his contortions.

Or you will decide perhaps to have no gimmicks other than your own distinctive and utterly charming personality—and why not? If Bob Hope and Tony Hancock did it, why not you? But let us consider those two names more closely: Bob Hope's image is that of a cad, a braggart and a bounder. He presents us with a man who is a bit of a coward who will almost certainly fail to get the girl. When a *persona* as complicated as this

is presented to us clearly defined we know how given situations and events
will affect him; we know what he is likely to enjoy and what he is likely
to hate; the more interesting and many-sided the character, the more
fascinated we shall be in what he has to say. Even then he may well surprise
us by doing the unexpected—as when Stan Laurel would suddenly turn on
Oliver Hardy and belt him one—but as long as the characterization is
consistent, solidly based and maintained with integrity we shall stay
faithful.

Hancock was the supreme comic genius. He showed us a *persona* so
complex—innocent but knowing, naïve but sly, moral but lascivious, edu-
cated but ignorant—that the whole of Britain revelled in his weekly dis-
comfitures on radio, and later on television. But it was on stage that the
true magic of his art was revealed. This was a giant personality; large
mobile features whose slightest change could be seen at the back of the
gallery; that wonderfully genteel surburban accent with an ever-lurking
hint of hysteria. His performances reminded me of everything I have ever
read about Dan Leno, in that it was the soul of the man that communi-
cated itself so directly to everyone present. It was the soul of a man
constantly at war with all the little ignominies of life, the frustrations and
upsets and worries and problems which we all suffer and which he made
seem so funny. But he was never silly: we would soon have lost patience
and sympathy with a man who was just foolish. He tried so hard always
to do the right thing, to be the gentleman, to make something of himself—
all to no avail. The droop of his mouth as he (and we) realized that Fate
had dealt him another one off the bottom of the pack was the richest
comic experience imaginable; his sketches would go awry, his impersona-
tions wouldn't fool a cat, his dramatic recitations would be laughed at,
but still he would try and try again with desperate earnestness, gathering
up the tattered remnants of his dignity like a moth-eaten shield.

I have said that Tony Hancock's art had to be seen live to be fully
appreciated, and I think this is true of many comics. Television so often
seems to diminish personality, possibly because in the case of a man used to
playing large rooms and huge variety theatres it cannot be adjusted to the
size of the screen image that will appear in the living-rooms of the nation,
and thereby is paradoxically reduced in impact. It is significant that with
very few exceptions the most popular television comedy shows have been
situation series rather than variety shows as such, starring actors rather
than comics—Michael Crawford, Harry H. Corbett and Wilfred Bram-
bell, Arthur Lowe, Richard Briers and Penelope Keith being examples.

So, what posture will you adopt? Are you going to be a Bertie Wooster
or an Alf Garnett? Are you tall or short? Fat or thin? Bald or hirsute?
Can you dance and/or sing well? Do you have a large nose and a squint?
Have you a funny face and a squeaky voice? Or are you pleasantly bland?

I have an averagely English sort of face without any distinguishing
peculiarities, but experience has taught me that there is one grimace I can
pull which gets a laugh. I use this sparingly—certainly not more than once
per act—and with sharp unexpectedness on a tag-line or perhaps when
answering a heckler, thus producing a very satisfactory reaction. I mention

this because it took me some years to pluck up the courage to try raising a laugh by purely facial means; you may care to consider your own equipment's potential in this light. Have you any funny faces, funny walks or mannerisms of speech which infallibly convulse your friends and relations at parties? These eccentricities, suitably broadened out, might work just as well on stage. For instance, a friend of mine, the actor and Music Hall comic John Hollis, is wont to say in his act: "I went to the barber's the other day. The barber said to me, 'Short back and sides?' I said, 'No, just give me a re-tread!' " And he removes his hat revealing a totally hairless dome, to shrieks of mirth.

Ronnie Corbett is a well-known exponent of the short of stature gag; the late and very great Norman Evans had a face which seemed to fold up (he removed his teeth to facilitate this, although Les Dawson seems to be produce the same effect with his teeth in!); Nat Jackley has a very long neck which he exaggerates with eccentric movements; Fred Emney's girth materially aids his country squire image; Groucho Marx's moustache was even painted on his face in films; Bernie Winter's rabbit grin is an impressionist's gift; Tommy Cooper's apparent haplessness and shambling gait make us laugh before he says or does anything at all, and Frankie Howerd's lugubrious face and confused manner hide a razor-sharp awareness.

Are you going to be regional or non-specific (i.e. Southern)? Bernard Miles used to work as the "Uncrowned King of the Chiltern Hills" and told rustic stories; Ken Dodd's frequent references to Knotty Ash and Fazakerley place him firmly as a Lancashire Lad; Wyn Calvin and Max Boyce are very definitely Welsh, and no Irish or Scottish comic lets us forget his place of origin for one second.

Are you going to be gormless like Ken Goodwin or knowing like Frank Carson? Bouncy like Brian Marshall or put-upon like Mrs Shufflewick? However you decided to put yourself across, be different, be distinctive and be positive. If your material isn't original, you must be.

Conclusion

Having worked out your routine you must learn it thoroughly. More than once I have seen a comic tell the same gag twice, or muff a tag-line, or get a story hopelessly confused because he didn't take this elementary precaution.

Keep a strong impetus in your delivery and in the pauses between gags —that first contact with your audience must never be broken. I always think that performing a patter routine is like running the 100-yard dash; you must lean forward all the time or else you will fall flat on your face. This effort of concentration, of erecting and maintaining a psychic bridge between yourself and your audience, is the reason why so many comics finish their acts bathed in sweat. It isn't the heat from the lights or the physical exertion involved, it is the sheer outpouring of self, of spirit, of that dynamism which excites attention and evokes affection.

Laughs must be capped before they die; the performer must monitor his act as he goes along; gags discarded or revamped according to reaction.

He must appear quite relaxed while in complete command, a combination which is perhaps the hardest aspect of the comic's job for the first can be acquired by experience but the second can only be put down to personality, that elusive quality which, like timing, has yet to be positively defined. Whether you can command an audience—whether you can retain their interest in what you have to tell them—is something you will only discover in practice. And if this sounds discouraging, perhaps I can raise your spirits by saying that it is perfectly possible for a personality to be developed and to expand. So if your first few attempts as a stand-up comic meet with less than overwhelming success, don't despair. Someone, somewhere will find you funny—sooner or later.

When you are going well telling funny stories seems the easiest way in the world to earn a living; when you're not it is the deadliest occupation known to civilized man.

To summarize: whatever individual characteristics you have that are special to you should be nurtured and cultivated and worked on, for it is those personal and unique quirks of appearance and personality that will mark you out as a comic with something different to offer. And that is never a bad thing.

OPENERS

If you are wearing eccentric clothes you will need to give your audience time to take in your appearance; a slow entrance can help, plus a pause when you reach the microphone. Some comics used to use a catch-phrase at this point to help establish themselves: Ken Platt with "I'll not take my coat off, I'm not stopping" and Frankie Howerd's "I'll just make myself comfy" while pulling at the seat of his trousers are examples. But catch-phrases are out of fashion at the moment, and audiences expect personality and charm as much as mere mechanical or technical comedy.

Try not to start with "Hello, how are you—all right?" This has been so heavily over-worked that my heart sinks when I hear a comic start with this threadbare opening; it shows a lack of imagination which is likely to extend to the remainder of his act. "Nice to be here" is another cliché for the start of many acts other than purely comic ones, but it is not to be despised since audiences always seem to believe it and it can lead you into remarks about the town or the hall you are playing in.

The following list of suggestions may spark off ideas of your own. Other openings are given in the acts themselves:

My God—people! (Fall flat on your back.)

I've just been appearing in a Jewish pantomine—Abe's in the Wood.

A dirty old tramp accosted me on the way here. He said to me, " 'Ere, guv, I 'aven't 'ad a bite for three days." So I bit him . . .

So this is (name of local new building) . . . it'll be nice when it's finished . . . no, I'm only joking. I like (name of actual hall, theatre or club) . . . as a (w)hole . . .

I got up out of a sick-bed to be here . . . my girl-friend's got 'flu.

Good evening. I won't call you ladies and gentlemen—you know who you are.

It's marvellous to be here . . . (to musical director) . . . where am I?

What do you think of the dinner jacket? I'm breaking it in for a waiter (or local colourful personality). Liberace was going to lend me one of his suits but it's still at the jeweller's.

What do you think of the suit? I got it backing a horse . . . backed it through Burton's window.

Thank you—keep applauding. I've got a very weak finish.

Thank you. And in conclusion . . .

This is a return engagement for me—I was here yesterday.

My name is Raquel Welch.

Thank you for your applause. For two pins I'd join in. It must be wonderful for you sitting out there watching me.

B

(When waiter passes with tray full of food or drinks.) Look at that—there's my salary on that tray . . . salary, hah! If this was China I'd be picketed by coollies . . .

Nice to see my kind of people here—skint.

As you can tell, I'm very well bred. Mind you, breeding's not everything . . . but it's a lot of fun . . . or so they tell me.

I should have been at my mother-in-law's funeral, but business before pleasure.

Do you know the guv'nor, Mr (name of manager)? He's the only man I know who suffers from an ingrowing wallet . . . still, you get a nice tan from the lights here.

Last night I was on the telly—when I'm drunk I'll sleep anywhere.

You've paid your money, you might as well make the best of it.

I'm working under a big disadvantage tonight—I'm sober.

We've got a mixed bag for you this evening. She should be here about half-past nine.

To Band

Well, boys . . . *boys!!!* . . . haven't seen you in Oxford Street lately (or local).

There they are, Ivy Benson's rejects . . . she's a girl, though, that one . . . no, not that one (pointing to leader) . . . oh, I don't know, though . . . I have to be careful what I say—he's a devil with his handbag . . .

Our conductor has just been playing with a sextet. The other five were all girls and you can't get a sexier tet than that.

He can do something with his baton that Yehudi Menhuin can't do with his violin . . . stir his tea.

There they are, the Stockwell Stompers (or local), the only band I know where the drummer carries the tune. But I must be tactful—they're all qualified plumbers, you know. Oh yes, there's nothing (name of leader) doesn't know about wiping a joint, I can tell you.

They will now play the Stiffening Movement from Rigor Mortis . . .

They will now play the Waltz Theme from King Kong.

Here we have Knuckles O'Reilly and his Ditch Diggers.

Have you noticed the way they always laugh at my jokes? That's only fair —I always laugh at their playing.

After Noisy Introduction

All right, all right, we know you're there . . . you won't get any extra for that, you know.

This is a fine time to practise.

To Pianist

A long time ago he used to play the violin. That was when Max Jaffa was a tangerine.

Here he is, the King of Swing—Albert Pierrepoint.

He's a bachelor of music and a father of six.

He plays with great feeling . . . feeling for the right note.

He's our relief pianist—it's such a relief when he stops.

Here he is—(first name) what-the-hell-are-the-black-notes-for? (surname)!
Tonight he will be playing as never before—in tune.
Last week he played the Palladium, tonight he plays the piano.
He not only plays the pianoforte but also the euphonium, the harmonium,
  the pandemonium, the B flat Hoover and the DDT spray.
He loves classical music. I said to him, "Do you like Handel's Largo?"
  and he said, "I never drink anything else."

CLOSERS

The simplest get-off is to mark your exit music with the tag-line of the final gag and to go off waving and blowing kisses—the music will naturally be bright and fast. But for goodness' sake do too little rather than too much. If you hear shouts of "More!" during your bows then you know you have succeeded. (It isn't a bad idea, by the way, to have an encore gag ready.) If a gag gets a much bigger laugh than you have anticipated, and you doubt whether your concluding material will be up to this—cut and get off while you're ahead; but warn the band-leader beforehand.

Don't take your bows too quickly: an audience likes to know that its appreciation is in turn appreciated by the recipient of their applause, so don't bow too perfunctorily—calls are all *part* of an act and not an unnecessary adjunct.

I'd love to stay but we're already into injury time.
I must go now—if I'm not back by eleven the wife lets out my room.
I must go now—if I'm not in bed by eleven I'm going home.
I must go now—my mother-in-law's out on parole/home on leave.
I must go now—I've got a fair bit to do at the office.
I must go now—I've got to get back to Elmer's End (or local) and he's a very demanding lad.
I'll go now while I'm winning.
Well, you're getting tired, so . . .

For Encore Stamp on the Floor, Look Down and Shout
Leave the keys, Charlie—I'll lock up.
I'd like to thank (local personality) without whose help it would all have been—so much easier.
I'll leave you with a little thought: should a couple about to be married be frank and earnest with each other—or should one of them be a girl?
I'll leave you with a little thought: Confucius, he say—man who make love to girl on side of hill, not on level.
Do be careful as you go home. Did you know that one man is knocked down in (local) every five minutes? And he's getting pretty fed up with it.
I've got some good news for you—it's pouring outside . . . no, I'm only kidding—it's snowing.
You've been a challenge, and you've won.
I must go, I've got another booking—next March.
I'd love to see you all again—(looking at difficult table or heckler) or most of you.

The management have made me a presentation—a ten-pound tin of baked
beans. I'd just like to say that I'm—deeply moved.
Thanks for coming—we need the money.
We'll never forget you . . . no matter how hard we try.

When Closing With a Song
Don't give me a key, maestro—I'll let myself in.
Give us a quick archipelago—I love these Italian cars.
Start pedalling, Vicar . . .
I'm going to sing at you now—I don't know why, you've done nothing to
me, but here is a little chor*arse* entitled:
Get off the gas stove, Granny, you're too old to ride the range.
I used to kiss you on the lips, but now it's all over.
Careless Hands, or Cry of the Wild Goose.
Who hit Annie on the fanny with a flounder?
If I had to do it all over again, I'd do it all over you.
I met her in the fog—and missed.
I can't get over a girl like you, so *you* get up and make the tea.
She was only the mayor's daughter, but she wouldn't let the borough
surveyor.
She was only a footballer's daughter, but she liked her 'Uddersfield.
She was only a farmer's daughter, but she wouldn't let the combine
harvester.
Father's swallowed the thermometer, now he's dying by degrees.
The song of the Irish chiropodist—Me Fate is in Your Hands.
A song written by Admiral Lord Nelson entitled Please Don't Talk
About Me—One Eye's Gone.
Cleopatra tried to stay aloof, but you should have seen Julius Caesar.
Here's a little number I wrote myself while waiting for a laugh in (local).

For Community Singing
If you don't sing up I'm coming down there with a big whip . . . oh, no,
you might enjoy that . . .
I want each and every one of you to open your mouth and really throw
yourself into it.
Big breaths . . .
Open your vowels, now.
We have a party of midwives in the gallery, and we're expecting a really
good delivery from them.
For the one who sings the best there will be a really wonderful prize:
(look at piece of paper) a diving suit . . . (look again at paper more
carefully) . . . oh no—a divan suite.
I'd like you to raise your voices in harmony, in unison, and with any luck,
in tune.
If you can't sing, take your shoes off and hum.
That's right, dear, take your coat off . . . have a night out . . . spread a
little happiness . . .

Where Song-sheets are Provided

Have you all got your song-sheets? . . . Printed in this week's language
which happens to be English—I hope that suits you all . . . have you
got them? Please wave your white forms at me . . . thank you, it gets a
little stuffy in here . . . now, can you all read? . . . so much for com-
pulsory education . . . and can you all count? . . . then let us turn our
attention to number X, hymns ancient and decrepit, and entitled . . .

The next song is number X on your race-cards . . .

You start pedalling, Vicar, and we'll catch you on the upthrust.

LAUGHS

Many comics have a tendency to become self-conscious about their technique. Frankie Howerd's "I have to laugh meself and I'm in it!" may be excused since that is a funny remark in itself, but Frank Carson's constant reiteration of "It's the way I tell 'em" and Charlie Williams' "Ee, that's a belter!" become tedious all too soon.

Allow your audience to discover how funny you are for themselves; let your act have the appearance of a friendly chat between intimate pals so that the humour arises out of your *persona* with apparent spontaneity. Larry Grayson is a delightful example of a comic who doesn't seem to tell stories as such; his humour grows and flowers without bullying or badgering his audience as he recounts the events of his day, just as though we were all having a companionable drink in our local.

However, having said that, I offer here four examples of fillers which can be useful to help quieten an audience down after a particularly protracted laugh:

Did you enjoy that? For two pins I'd tell it again . . .
I'd tell you more jokes but you'd only laugh.
Laugh? I thought my trousers'd never dry.

After Risqué Story
My mother told me that one.

No Laughs

The reasons for poor response are many and varied: the audience may be physically cold, they may not be able to hear you properly, they may be drunk, they may be sober, they may be too old, too young, you may be on too early in the programme, you may be on too late, the seating may be uncomfortable. Or perhaps your audience just doesn't like you because your personality is unsympathetic and/or you are using the wrong material. Never mind, you must smile all the more winningly—smiling is a very important part of any comic's act—and plough on: suddenly they may decide they'll like you after all and give you an enormous hand when you finish, by way of apology.

Old folks like their comedy slow, broad and lavatorial; they like long stories, and jokes about knickers and bedpans, but not jokes about drugs or homosexuality. Teenagers like jokes about drugs and homosexuality, also zany, madcap humour and visual gags—but, like the pensioners, they are a little slow on the uptake. British audiences in their twenties seem to

go for speed, wit and sophistication; from the thirties it is undoubtedly
filth which raises the biggest laughs, whether you call it "honest vulgarity"
or "adult humour". Politics and money are also reliable subjects for most
age and class groupings.

But if, having taken all precautions with your act you are still not getting
your laughs, what are you to do? One remedy is to cut to your sure-fire
boffo gags, then when you feel you have retrieved the situation you can
put in the omitted material. But it is probably better, as and when the
laughs start coming, to press on. If your earlier stories weren't making
'em laugh they probably needed cutting anyway. Or you can give up en-
tirely and go into your closing song. This is safe, but there will be no chance
to experiment if you give up the ghost. Sooner or later you must persevere
with your rehearsed gags, just to see whether you can do it. It will be
hideously embarrassing if you can't, and indeed there is always a strong
whiff of embarrassment in all patter acts, but it is just this element of
danger which makes the solo turn so exciting.

The one-liners listed below should only be used with extreme caution,
when you know that an audience is on your side even when they are not
laughing very much. If you are really dying it is better not to draw attention to the fact. A comic of my acquaintance bases his whole act on telling
appalling jokes and then reacting off the groans or boos or lack of response, but only a performer of considerable experience and rock-hard
nerve could get away with it.

I'm going to remember every last damn one of you.
I've paid for this material and I'm going to use it.
My mother told me there would be nights like this.
You may not like me now but later on you'll learn to hate me.
Me English . . .
These are the jokes.
I suppose fate is against me—people just don't like handsome, virile men.

Small Laugh
I'm glad you both came.
I know you're out there, I can hear you breathing.
Please yourselves.
Was it something I said?
So this is where the good jokes come when they die.
They loved me in the dressing-room.
Thank you for that burst of apathy.
Hasn't it gone quiet . . .? Must be a lousy act on.
I just threw that one in. I needn't have bothered.

To Pianist
That shut 'em up.
We'll be home early tonight.
Are you sure Ted Rogers started like this?
That was my best joke—from here it's all downhill.

You try and get your money back . . .

Late Laughs
Late laughs are the comic's joy for it shows that his audience is attending to him. But the following should be used sparingly, or they become wearisome. Keep your cool at all times even under the grossest provocation; an audience laughing too much can be almost as dangerous as one laughing too little, since exhaustion can deaden an audience's capacity to laugh just as surely as the desperation of an unfunny comic, and the gaiety will change to a sullen resentment.

A Single Laugh
It's you and me against the rest, brother (or sister).
Laugh with the rest or get out.
No solo titters, please.
You'll have to come again tomorrow.
Am I going too fast for you? I'm sorry, but I want to get home before the pills wear off.
Have you just worked it out, sir? Well, put it back . . .
Pass it along.
It's there if you look for it . . . not now, dear, later please!
You'll have to be quicker, it's a very long show.
Is there an echo in here?
With this material you've got to be alert. It creeps up on you like tight trousers.
Here I'm doing comedy, there tragedy.

A Single Woman's Laugh
Thank you, Mother.
Are you being interfered with, madam? If not, why don't you move over here—I'm sure these gentlemen will oblige.

HECKLE-STOPPERS

To respond successfully to heckling is the surest way for a comic to ingratiate himself with his audience. British audiences especially seem to love repartee, which is possibly why there tends to be far more heckling in this country than in others. Perhaps it is our island tradition of street-corner soap-box oratory which has fostered this custom—and the House of Commons has been renowned for centuries for the vigour of its debates.

One caveat: don't be too savage, especially at the beginning of the show. You want to show that you possess the superior wit, but to do so it shouldn't be necessary to grind your heckler into little pieces.

Men

To Man Shouting Incomprehensibly

I beg your pardon, sir . . . ? You don't mind me calling you sir, do you? . . . it's just in fun.

Would you mind repeating that, sir? (if he does his comment will almost always fall flat) I see . . . do you know any jokes? . . . (beware—someone may shout out "do you?" and you must have a solid bofferoo ready to prove that you do).

I beg your pardon, madam . . . ?

I'm sorry, I couldn't hear you—I was talking.

Why don't you go down to the morgue and tell them you're ready?

You'll have to excuse him—he's being himself tonight.

Why don't you move closer to the wall—that's plastered already.

If I'd known I was doing a double-act I'd have asked for more money.

Hello, liquor mortis has set in.

I get paid for making a fool of myself—what's your excuse?

He's suffering from bottle fatigue.

You're making a big mistake . . . like your father before you.

Are you with anyone or are you alone in that suit . . . ?

I hate that tie . . .

He must be a bundle of fun at home.

Just because you're impotent don't take it out on me.

Women

I would advise extreme caution when responding to lady hecklers. They don't often indulge in shouting out in public and when they do are quite possibly drunk, and a drunk heckler is always difficult to quieten since he or she will be insensible to any feeling of irritation which may be manifested by the audience. And your wittiest sallies will probably be countered with a surly "—off!". But whether drunk or sober, lady hecklers must be dealt with very circumspectly, since British audiences dislike any lack of gallantry, so your biting response must be tempered with colossal charm. Don't forget to smile!

I don't know why she keeps on at me—I left the money on the mantel-
    piece . . .
What's the matter? Someone pinch your broom?
I don't know what she does for a living but she's got a telly on the ceiling.
Did anyone ever tell you you were beautiful and what were they drinking
    at the time?
I don't know what she does for a living but she's got corns on her shoulder-
    blades.
Mother! You should be out front parking the cars.
Hello, it's Miss Stomach Pump of 1946.
Yes, sir?

To Woman in Front
I wouldn't sit there, love, we can all see your roots.

Either:

Would you mind having your nervous breakdown somewhere else?
I wonder if he/she goes on like this when he's/she's having sex . . .
Please sir/madam, you're embarrassing your daughter/son . . .
I've never believed in Darwin's theory but looking at you I'm not so sure.
Why don't you go home—your cage'll be cleaned out by now.
You don't think I'm funny? I laughed when you came in.
Keep Britain tidy—get out.
If ever there's a price on your head—take it.
Anyone got a flit gun?

To Bearded Man
Thank you, sir. I like the beard . . . very naval. Haven't I seen you on a
    packet of Players? Of a packet of something . . .

LATECOMERS AND MISCELLANEOUS

Drawing attention to latecomers is always popular, but it is as well to establish yourself as the likable, lovable chap that you are before taking the rise out of anyone. I would also counsel restraint; once you have made remarks to, say, three latecomers it is best to carry on with the show and leave further stragglers unnoticed.

Some of the following may also be of use after an interval:

To Party
Is this your annual do?
Latecomers, I see . . . Tillings are so unreliable these days.
Ah, it's Sir Thomas Lipton's tea-party.

To Couple
Is that the wife? . . . novelty night.
         . . . oh, no—she's got a box of chocs.
         . . . couldn't you find a clean shirt for him, dear?
         . . . or is this a pleasure trip?
Is that feller with you, dear? . . . Never mind, the evening may improve.
Why are you late? Or is that an embarrassing question?

To Women
Hello, girls . . . trade bad?
         . . . stood up again?
         . . . did you turn the gas off?

To Men
Hello, boys—no luck in (local High Street)?
You two gentlemen together? . . . I see . . .

Bald-headed Man
Would you mind sitting down quickly, sir—the light from your head is shining in my eyes . . . I bet he combs his hair with a sponge.

To Woman in Striking Coat or Dress
I like the coat—who shot the couch?
I've seen you before, haven't I? . . . yes—ten years ago at the (local theatre) . . . I remember the dress!

To Woman in Low-cut Dress
Don't get hiccups in that dress, will you, dear?

Think of a number between one and ten . . . six? You lose—take your
clothes off.

I've seen nothing like that since I was weaned . . .

I don't know why, I suddenly fancy a milk stout . . .

When are you going to buy the rest of that dress?

General
What time do you call this?

Do you have a seat? . . . and somewhere to put it? (If there is a response
of "No!") . . . well, do your coat up and no-one will notice.

Did your horse throw a shoe?

Don't be embarrassed—everyone's looking at you.

You're early for tomorrow's show.

Would you like us to start again? (If response is "Yes!") do a lightning
and semi-articulate run-down of the show to that point.)

Have you got a note? A fiver will do.

Good evening—we did wait for you, but we thought we'd have the show
first and eat afterwards.

Good evening—you have come to the right meeting? You have come to be
saved?

No, don't stand up—make 'em jump . . . you're nearly there . . . on the
last lap.

Latecomers, I see . . . pay no attention—just pretend you're enjoying
yourselves.

We did wait for you . . .

Nothing good on the telly tonight?

To Anyone Walking Out Very Soon After the Show Has Started
I never forget a back—I don't mind 'em going that way, it's when they
start coming this way I get worried.

There goes the only man with taste.

Hello—the critics are in!

Had enough already? Chicken . . .

To Man Leaving Any Time
He'll be back in a wee while.

He'll be back in a couple of shakes.

He's just going to have one on the house.

Leave your pencil behind, please. We've just had it white-washed.

You know where it is? Ladies on right and gentlemen's on left. If you get
them confused it may be embarrassing but think of the friends you'll
make . . .

Try not to be long.

To Women Leaving
Why is it they always go in pairs?

To People Returning
Feel better now? . . . Yes, now you can relax, can't you?
Do you know your shoes are wet?
Could you hear us out there? . . . we could hear you in here.

To Couple Leaving
Where are you two going? Like animals, some people . . .
Can't wait, eh? Turned her on for you, have I, son . . .?

To Woman
No, don't pick your nose, love.
That's a smashing turn of leg you've got there, dear . . . pity it's only the one.

To Party of Women
May I say how nice it is to see you ladies here. What I say is, a theatre/club/restaurant without ladies is like a garden without flowers . . . (wait for "aaaah's") . . . what a creep!

On Unexpected Laugh
Unexpected laugh—check flies (suit action to the word).

After Interval
Are you enjoying yourselves . . . why, what are you doing?

For Location Near River
I know some people are a little worried, as we're so near the river here, about the dangers of flooding, but I can assure you that the management have installed—at ENORMOUS expense—a flood warning device. So should there be the slightest chance of flooding, this device takes the form of a flashing buoy . . . so should you see the buoy flash . . . uncontrollably . . . what you have to do is—move against the walls and give me a clear run for the door. I can't swim a stroke.

To Couple
Is this your husband? . . . where are you from, love? . . . Really? Did you know there was a survey done there recently which shows that fifty per cent of the married women in (wherever) are unfaithful to their husbands . . . yes! And the Archbishop of Canterbury wrote a letter to the other fifty per cent. And do you know what he said . . .? No? . . . Didn't you get one?
How to cope with birthdays, wedding anniversaries, raffles, etc., is dealt with in my book *It Gives Me Great Pleasure* (Samuel French).

If You Fluff
Sorry I'm breaking these teeth in for the dog.
That's the last time I get my teeth by mail order.

To Waiter Passing With Well-filled Tray
There's my salary on that tray.
Is that wine or plasma?

In Restaurant
Don't have the tomato soup—the chef's a vampire.
Have a nice meal? It should be good—I've been in the kitchen and twenty thousand flies can't be wrong.
Have you tried the steak here? The chef's a marvel—he can rustle up a steak with his eyes shut . . . and that's the best way to eat it.

In Response to a Shouted Request
I'm sorry—we only accept requests on the appropriate form, which in this establishment is a ten pound note.

If You are Handed a Note
I'm told that a gentleman's wallet has been handed in to our receptionist, Helen—Miss Helen Hunt. So if any gentleman has lost his wallet, he can go to Hell 'N Hunt.

On St Patrick's Night or for Irish Party
Did you know we have an honoured guest from Ireland here tonight? It is none other than an authentic leprechaun—he's sitting just here. He's invisible, of course . . . (hold out hand) charming little chap—jump on my hand . . . that's it . . . (move to woman in front) . . . would you like to tickle him under the chin? . . . (after she does so indicate a figure much larger with your other hand) . . . actually, he's this tall, but he enjoyed that . . .

To Out-of-Town Visitors
I hear things are looking up in (wherever) . . . they're sending a missionary from (local).
That's a lovely part of the world. I was talking to a woman from there the other day and I said, "I should imagine the only trouble with living there are the rates." She said, "Oh, we don't have rates in (wherever) . . . only mice." (Use posh accent.) I went there once but it was shut.
You come from (wherever)? . . . a very wise move.
I spent a year there . . . one Wednesday afternoon . . . no, I'm only kidding —I used to have relations there. I won't say who with but it was a wonderful summer.
Once when I was there I found myself passing the rent office, so I thought I'd pop in—just to see if it was like mine, 'cos I live in (local posh area), you see. And there was this woman, in the rent office, standing there with a five pound note stuck in each ear. So I said to the chap behind the counter, "What's all this, then? This woman with a five pound note stuck in each ear?" He said, "Oh, pay no attention—she's ten pound in arrears ('er ears)."

At Interval

All drinks will be free—provided you stick to water.

There will be a free drink for everyone tonight. Yes, a free drink with every two pound bag of crisps.

The band and I will retire behind the scenes where we shall talk about you.

We had hoped to close the first half of the show with the dance of the three virgins . . . but unfortunately . . . they've broken their contract . . . so we'll see you in fifteen minutes.

FIVE-MINUTE PATTER ACT—ONE

Isn't it hot, eh? Phew—sweltering! I tell you, on the way here I saw a tree **1**
chasing a dog . . .
(*This is a bigger laugh than you might imagine, so give it a chance.*)

Had your holidays, then? I went abroad this year. I love being abroad . . . **2**
mind you, I prefer being a chap . . . but there it is, you can't have everything.
(*Give this a little time also to sink in. The last phrase is just a throwaway
while the point of the gag sinks in.*)

I went to the south of France. Beautiful weather, lovely beaches, marvellous hotel—that night I arrived I went into the dining-room, the waiter
gave me a menu—all in French. So I looked at it and said, "I'll have a bit
of that." He said, "You'll be lucky—that's the manager!" I said, "All **3**
right, then, have you got frog's legs?" He said, "Yes"; I said, "Well, hop **4**
into the kitchen and get us a steak!" Then, that night, I'd just gone to bed
when the manager banged on my bedroom door. He said, "Have you got **5**
a woman in there?" I said, "No"—so he threw me one in . . . very nice . . .
(*This paragraph should be delivered rapidly—don't give 'em a chance to grow
cold on you: the first two gags are solid so these three will reap the benefit
of the goodwill you've built up. Now you can relax a little.*)

But of course I can speak the lingo a little, you know. Just enough to get
by—just a few well-known phrases and sayings, like . . . (*act "thinking"*)
. . . "Pas de deux"; (*let the audience think of the correct translation, then:*) **6**
that means "Father of twins". Then there's "Coq au vin"—that's "chicken
on a lorry". "Hors de combat"—"two tarts fighting"; and "Le petite
chose" . . . that means your flies are undone!
(*The last translation should be delivered very rapidly with a shout of triumph.*)

But I met this lovely little dolly over there. What a darling—French, she
was. They called her Patti de Faux Pas. I first saw her in this little bistro—
I'd just popped in for a drink, so I said to the garçon . . . (*slight pause: if
there's a laugh repeat*) . . ."Here, garçon, get us a beer please." He said, **7**
"Oui, oui"; I said, "I'd prefer draught Bass if you've got it." **8**
(*"I'd prefer, etc." must come swiftly on "Oui, oui". This is one of those gags
which a British audience loves—they see the tag coming a mile off and enjoy
it all the more.*)

But there was Patti sitting all by herself, looking lonely. There was a band

C

playing so I sent the gar*k*on over to ask her for a dance. They made a
9 lovely couple . . . (*don't dwell on this one, since it is well enough known, but
gives your audience a breather*) . . . of course, these French girls have
10 marvellous dress sense, don't they? And Patti got more out of a dress than
any other girl I know . . . but she was a very nice girl—the salt of the earth.
And you should have seen her shaker. I said to her once, "Do you know
what virgins eat for breakfast?" She said, "No." (*Slight pause, then crack
in with:*) I said, "I thought so!" But she was very good to her mother . . .
11 (*pause for the titter which this usually gets, then:*) she never goes home . . .

But talking of languages I picked up a Spanish bit—I mean a bit of
Spanish on the old Costa Packet last year. Not much—just enough to
12 know that mañana means tomorrow and pyjama means tonight!
(*Mañana is pronounced man-yana: this is a bigger laugh than you might
expect.*)

And in Germany all you need to know is "Ich liebe dich" . . . (*the phrase
usually gets a titter, so give it time*) . . . which roughly translated means
13 "I'm very fond of Richard" . . . (*This sometimes takes a little time for them
to work out, so let it breathe before you go into the first story—so far the
act has been quick cracks.*)

14 But coming over on the ferry—I've gone off flying ever since I went on a
plane with an outside loo—I found this gorgeous little brunette in the
bunk above mine. In the middle of the night she whispered, "Are you
awake?" (*All the dialogue should be said in a sexy, conspiratorial whisper,
except for the tag.*) I said, "Yes." She said, "I'm cold . . . wiil you get
me another blanket?" I said, "If you're cold, love, why don't we—pretend we're married? Just for the night?" She said, "All right," I said,
15 "Well, get your own ruddy blanket!"
(*This is a totally unexpected tag so the build-up can be dwelled on, with the
tag rapped out curtly.*)

(*In contrast, the next gag should be delivered swiftly.*)
But I did have a laugh coming through Customs. There was this very
elegant French woman in front of me; the Customs man opened up her
case, rummaged around inside and found six pairs of panties. "What's all
16 this, then?" he said. She said, "Sunday, Monday, Tuesday, Wednesday,
Thursday, Friday." He said, "What about Saturday?" She said, "Oh, la,
la . . ." Then came this stout party from Lancashire. In *her* case she had
twelve pairs of red flannelette drawers! The Customs man said, "What's
all this, ma?" She said, "January, February, March, April . . .!"
(*The French woman should be given a sultry French accent, to contrast with
the stout party from Lancashire—or any region whose accent you can do best.*)

Mind you, if you want a really exciting holiday—a really exciting holiday
—(*the repetition is to calm your audience down and compose their minds for
17 the next gag*) you want to go to Africa on safari. This couple were on safari

beating a path through the jungle when a huge lion suddenly burst out of the bush, seized the wife in his jaws and started carrying her off! (*Pause for the plot-line to sink in and the situation savoured.*) She yelled to her husband, "Shoot! Shoot!" He said, "I can't . . . (*pause*) . . . I've run out of film!"
(*The tag should be spoken with an agonized expression.*)

By the way, for any ladies on the Pill, the time is now half-past nine . . . **18**
(*pause*) . . . well, you can't be too careful . . . did you know that every fifth child born into the world today is Chinese? So watch yourself, ladies . . . **19**
(*These two gags are just throwaways, to give the act a gear-change.*)

My brother went to Butlin's for a couple of weeks this summer. Well, **19a**
actually he was only there for seven days—they gave him a week off for good behaviour . . . he's a jerry-builder, my brother . . . married a chambermaid . . . what you might call a marriage of convenience . . . **20**
(*This is a "silly" type gag, which you might acknowledge in your demeanour; but I have found it successful none the less.*)

I remember a saucy little chambermaid once in a Manchester hotel. Now there's a lot of unpleasant things said about Manchester with all that rain. **21**
I don't believe it myself, though last time I went to Belle Vue the zoo keeper was building an ark . . .
(*The reference to Manchester can be changed to a suitable area if required; if you want to keep it strictly local you can name one of the local hotels. If you use a different town there are the standard insults such as: "I like——as a (w)hole" or "I spent a year in ——, one Tuesday afternoon . . .")*
Anyway, at this hotel, this very cute little chambermaid came in to my room to turn the bedclothes down. She said, "Would you like a cup of tea or something in bed in the morning?" I said, "A cup of tea or something in bed would be very nice . . . say about eight o'clock?" So at seven I was up, had a shave and a shower and a quick squirt round with the Brut, put **22**
on my shortie pyjamas and a clean night-cap . . . (*pause for whatever this might bring*) . . . and got back into bed. At eight on the dot there was a tap on the door. "Come in!" I said (*this said with joyful anticipation*); the door opened and in came a feller! With a tray! I said, "Where's the chambermaid?" (*Pause.*) He said, "I dunno, but the teapot comes from Staffordshire . . ."

22a Been a funny sort of day, hasn't it? . . . what a wonderful day for shoving a cucumber through someone's letter-box and shouting, "The Martians have landed!" . . .
(*This can be a very big laugh indeed so wait for it.*)

23 No, but it has been a funny day. I saw a feller in the High Street (or local) this afternoon—he was wearing a tam o'shanter on his head, a kilt, a sporran—he wasn't wearing those on his head—and he had on a plaid shawl, he had a dagger in his socks, and he was carrying a set of bagpipes under his arm. So I went up to him and said, "Here, Taffy . . . is anything worn under that kilt?" And he said, "Och, naw, everything's in pairfect wurrrking arrderrr . . .!"
(*"Here, Taffy . . ." can be repeated if the laugh justifies it. The tag-line, spoken in broad Scots, should be spoken slowly to ensure its intelligibility.*)

24 (*Puff on cigar.*) This cigar came from Havana . . . (*cough*) . . . I think it had a rough trip . . . I also smoke a pipe . . . I like a good shag . . . That reminds me—

25 This couple went to a fancy dress ball dressed up as a cow—a cow! And the husband went in the front of the cow because *he* smoked a pipe, you see. They lived in the country not far from the village hall where the ball was being held, and on the way it started raining, so the wife said, "Let's get in the skin, save us getting wet." And the husband said, "OK—and let's take a short cut across the field." So they did, they put on the skin and took a short cut across the field. They'd got about half-way across when they heard krrrump-krrrump-krrrump! And the wife said, "What's that? . . . (*pause for chuckles as the audience begins to comprehend where the story is leading*) . . . he said, "I dunno—you have a look. You've got the peephole . . ." So the wife looked and she said, "Blimey—there's a bull . . . it's charging right at us! What are we going to do?!" He said, "Well, I'm going to bend down and eat grass—you'd better brace yourself! Whoops!"
(*Allow a slight pause after "What are we going to do?!" then rap out the tag smartly; on the "Whoops!" arch backwards with your hands on your bottom.*)

26 Mind you, they are a very trying couple. Perhaps one day she'll let him.

27 Like another couple I know—a very unfortunate match. They're both Welsh, but she's Presbyterian and he's Sunday opening . . .
(*Pause after "Welsh" to let the information sink in.*)

Eventually she went to see her solicitor about getting a divorce. He said, "What are your grounds?" She said, "Adultery." He said, "Have you got **28** proof?" She said (*Welsh accent*), "Well, I'm pretty certain he's not the father of my child . . ."

Which reminds me of the two Welsh girls talking, and one said, "I hear Myfanwy's getting married." "Oh?" said the other, "she's pregnant, then." **29** The first girl said, "No, she's not pregnant." "Oooh," says the other, "there's posh!"
(*"No, she's not pregnant"* should be said in tones of indignation.)

This little girl kept sucking her thumb so her mother said to her, "If you keep doing that you'll swell up and burst!" A couple of days later the little girl's out in the street with her mother when she sees a woman about eight **30** months' gone. The little girl goes up to her and says, "I know what you've been doing!"
(*The tag-line should be delivered in a little girl's voice with intense satisfaction—there is nothing children like better than ticking off other children or, as in this case, adults. This recognition of a psychological truth enhances any gag.*)

I love kids, though—I've got a little boy of my own. Born and bred in London, but one day we took him out into the country for the first time— I love visiting the countryside, don't you? Watching all those couples on the verge . . . but anyway, we were having a look round this beautiful little **31** village when my kid saw a horse-drawn milk float. He'd never seen one of these before—he was fascinated. He walked up to the milkman and said, "Here, mister—you'll never get back to the depot." The milkman said, "Why not, sonny?" He said, "Your horse just lost all his petrol!"
(*The boy's voice should be indicated, but it isn't worth doing any accent for the milkman.*)

But there was a nice little pub in the village; I was having a swift gargle in the snug when this fellow came in selling tortoises. An old gaffer near me said, "How much be they, then?" The feller said, "To you, Dad, twenty pence." So the old chap bought one and toddled off. Half an hour later **32** he was back, the chap selling tortoises was still there, so the old codger went up to him and said, "Here, I'll have another one o' they meat pies but not so much crust on top . . ."
(*This time the countryman can have a thick accent.*)

Then a Temperance man came in, dishing out leaflets and telling us all about the evils of drink. Damn cheek, I thought, but then he ordered a large Scotch and took out a tin of worms. He put a couple in the Scotch, **33** and of course they wriggled about and then sank to the bottom. "There!" he said, "what does that prove?" And the old boy said, "If'n you get worms—drink whisky!"

But what a dolly of a barmaid they had there! What a figure—42, 24, 36! And that was only her head! (*Pause.*) No, really she had the most super
34 superstructure I've ever seen. I went back a week later—and she'd gone. I said to the landlord, "Where's the (*mime with hands*) girl, then?" He said, "Oh I had to get rid of her—she was always dipping in the till . . ."

35 But you don't want to drink too much of the beer here, you know—you won't get so much drunk as waterlogged . . .
(*This obviously only in a venue where there is a licence. Don't dwell on this gag—it's just a filler.*)

But there was a nasty tragedy in a brewery the other day—did you read about it? A chap fell in a vat of beer and was drowned. The foreman had
36 to go and tell his missus. She was very upset, of course, and she said, "Did he suffer much?" The foreman said, "I don't think so, missus, he got out twice to go to the gents!"

37 (*Puff and cough on cigar again.*) This is an expensive cigar—it was thrown out of a Rolls-Royce . . .

        She stood on the bridge at midnight,
        Her lips were all a-quiver;
38   She gave a cough, her leg fell off,
        And floated down the river.
(*This poem is just a nonsensical interlude between stories.*)

When I started in this business I took a correspondence course on how to be
39 a comedian in ten easy lessons. (*Pause.*) I only got the first one—don't know what happened to the other nine but my postman's playing the Palladium.

But I've done everything in show business, and I've been pretty successful,
40 though I say it myself. I've been in films, oh yes—did you see *Grease* with John Travolta? So, did I, jolly good film wasn't it?
(*Any currently popular film can be used here. Obviously "Did you see, etc.?" will be said as though you are about to say what part you played in the film. The tag will therefore be a downbeat throwaway.*)

41 Then there's pantomine—I've done them all . . . Robinson Beanstalk . . . and I'm a marvellous Dick in the Woods . . . even in a flea circus I stole the show, but there it is . . .
42 ("*But there it is*" *is just for continuity.*)

And I've travelled a lot—Australia . . . oh, yes, I've been down under . . . now and then . . . I tried surf riding on Bondi Beach but I couldn't get the
43 horse near the water. I've been to Bangkok . . . Hong Kong Kok . . . Singapore Kok . . . and that's a lot of (*minute pause*) travelling. In Hawaii
44 I watched the rotation of the crops. And I saw a mermaid there—yes, a mermaid. Lovely-looking creature—38, 24, and tenpence a pound.

And of course I'm pretty quick at picking up languages. I speak Urdu—
that's dialect of Bradford (*or local*), and a bit of Latin. "Sic transit gloria 45
mundi." That means Gloria should be all right by Monday.
(*All the preceding should be taken fairly fast. Pause slightly after "surf
riding".*)

But home's best—it's always nice to be home, isn't it? Because I'm very
patriotic, you know. Oh yes, I have the greatest respect for the Royal
Family. Well, they work so hard, don't they? A few weeks ago the Queen 46
went to pay a visit to this Military Hospital; she went along the wards, and
there, lying in one of the beds smartly at attention, his thumbs down the
seams of his sheets, was this old sweat from the Chelsea Pensioners. The
Queen stopped by his bed and said, "And how are you?" He said (*queru-
lous old man voice*), "I'm fine thank you, Your Majesty. Very gracious of
you to ask, Your Majesty."

The Queen said, "And why are you here?" He said, "Well, since you
ask, Your Majesty, I got boils on me botty!"

Well of course the CO and the matron and the staff were all furious—
he'd put a blight on the whole occasion. So after the Queen had gone they
all came running up to the old boy's bedside and said, "How dare you
talk to the Queen like that! You've disgraced us all!"

The old chap said, "Well, Her Majesty was kind enough to ask me what
was wrong wi' me, so I told her!"

The matron said, "Well you could have just said you were covered in
boils and left it at that. You didn't have to be so explicit."

Now, it so happened that a couple of weeks later the Prince of Wales
also paid a visit to the same hospital, and by a remarkable coincidence . . .
(*pause for audience to savour what is to come*) . . . he toured the same ward
and stopped by the same bed in which was lying the same old chap—at
attention, thumbs down by the seams in the sheets. "And how are you?"
asked the Prince. "I'm very well, Your Royal Highness. Very gracious of
you"—d'you like the accent?—(*pause for reaction*). "Very gracious of you
to ask, Your Royal Highness."

Then the Prince said, "And what is your trouble?" There was the CO,
the matron, the doctors, all the staff, so the old boy said, " 'Er—I'm
covered in boils, Your Royal Highness."

"Oh," said the Prince, "so they're spread since my Mother was here . . .!"
(*This gag gives plenty of scope for acting. Use any accent you like for the old
sweat; "By a remarkable coincidence" and "d'you like the accent?" are nice
booster laughs. Keep the story-line moving along, and you'll get a round of
applause.*)

47 Hasn't the weather been marvellous lately? Nice for the holidays—have you had yours yet? We went in April . . . well, I like to get in early while the sheets are still clean . . .

48 We went to the seaside this year—Carshalton Beeches . . . (*only of use in Surrey*).

49 No, actually we went to Brighton. It was a kind of sentimental journey, 'cos the wife and me spent our honeymoon there. We had a nice wedding —just a quiet family affair . . . just me, the wife and the kids . . . her mother
50 couldn't make it—she was on manoeuvres at the time.
(*Give a good wait after "the kids", since this is a nice laugh.*)

51 I remember saying to the vicar, "Do you believe in sex before the wedding?" And he said, "Not if it delays the ceremony . . ."

But I remember that first night so well. There we were, tucked up in bed with the moonlight streaming in through the holes in the ceiling . . . the
52 wife snuggled up to me and said, "Mr (*give your surname. This takes a little while to sink in so give it air and you will be surprised by the size of the laugh. If performing as chairman in an Old Time Music Hall say 'Mr Chairman . . .'*) . . ." well, we hadn't known one another long . . . she said,
53 "Mr ——, will you love me in the hereafter?" (*Pause, then rap out smartly on a rising inflection:*) I said, "If I don't get what I'm here after you'll be here after I've gone!"
(*This is one instance where you can laugh yourself after the tag.*)

So anyway, we decided to go back there this year. Had a nasty accident on the way, though. I was driving down this country lane when a big rooster flapped out through a gap in the hedge—straight under my front wheels! Killed it stone dead—terrible! The farmer's wife saw what happened, she came running over to me and started carrying on something alarming.
54 "Oh, my prize rooster! My prize rooster!" I said, "I'm sorry, love, I couldn't help it—he ran straight out in front of me." She said, "Oh, my prize rooster—you've killed him!" I said (*with a touch of asperity*), "Look, I'm sorry, dear, but it really wasn't my fault. I'll replace him if you like." She said, "All right—the hen-coop's just behind the barn . . ."
(*There must be a big contrast in the wife's manner before and after the offer to replace the rooster. Before she will be distraught with grief, after she will be very calm and matter-of-fact. This gag, by the way, is Barry Cryer's*

*fa urite—and as one of Britain's top script writers his opinion is not to be
sn zed at.*)

We couldn't keep out of trouble when we arrived at the hotel. We were
just walking up the steps to the front door when a big pigeon . . . (*indicate
the sky with a twinkle in your eye*) . . . a *big* pigeon he was . . . (*this should
get a few chuckles going as your audience anticipates what might be going
to happen*) . . . flying overhead, dropped his calling card right on the wife! **55**
Splat! All over her shoulder, down her new summer frock. She was
furious! She said to me, "Well, don't stand there laughing—do something!
Get some paper!" I said, "That wouldn't do any good—it'll be miles
away by now!"
(*As you say "miles away", look upwards and point in a travelling motion.*)

So we got up to the front door; there was this big old iron ring, so I gave
it a pull. The landlady opened the door, she said, "That'll be ten pounds."
I said, "What for?" She said, "You've just launched the lifeboat!" **56**

She was a funny woman, though. One day she met me in the hall when I
was on my own—the wife had just popped down the garden for a surprise
pea . . . well, we were doing for ourselves . . . and the landlady said,
"Would you like to come into my parlour and see my cat?" So I said, **57**
"All right, dear"—anything for a laugh. So she said, "Come in," and we
went into the parlour.
And there, on a mat in front of the fire, sat—a cat. She said, "This is
Tiddles." "Oh yes?" I said, "he's very nice." She said, "Yes, and he's
clever, too. He can play the piano!" (*Pause.*) I said, "Can he? The cat?
Tiddles?" She said, "Yes—would you like to see?" I said, "All right, **58**
love." So she said, "Tiddles!"—that's the cat . . . sitting on the mat . . .
she said, "Tiddles! Play!" And Tiddles got up—the cat—walked across
the room, jumped up on the piano stool, sat down on a pile of cushions,
and began to play! The cat! Tiddles! Fantastic—arpeggios, scales, runs
up and down the keyboard!
I said, "My goodness me, he does play well." She said, "Yes, he does,
doesn't he?" I said, "That's clever. And that piece he's playing: that's very
nice. I've never heard it before—did he write it himself?" She said, "Yes,
he did." I said, "It's marvellous. Have you had it orchestrated?" Well,
you've never seen a cat move so fast in all your life!
(*Plenty of time can be taken on this story. Act out the geography of the
parlour, with the cat on the mat to your left and the piano to your right.
Repetition of "cat", "mat", and especially "Tiddles" all help to keep the
laughs rippling. The tag must follow very quickly on "orchestrated"; after the
tag, as with the pigeon gag, your forefinger can indicate the cat's speedy exit.
The tag-line should also be spoken on a rising inflection.*)

Dear, oh dear, we did have a time. One day the wife sent me out to the
chemist—well, she'd been under a bit, you know how it is on honeymoon
. . . anyway, I got to the chemist's—old-fashioned place it was, with the **59**

manager, nice old boy, standing there in the doorway. "Good afternoon, sir," he said, "can I help you?" I said, "Yes, well, I need quite a few things,
60 actually." "Oh," he said, "do you have a list?" I said, "No, I always stand like this."

61 I said, "Well, first of all I'd like some rat poison." He said, "Oh, I'm terribly sorry, sir, we've just run out of rat poison. Why don't you try Boots?" I said, "I want to poison 'em, not kick 'em to death!"
(*The tag should follow very speedily on "Boots".*)

62 I said, "Have you got any Welsh letters?" He said, "What's a Welsh letter?" I said, "A French letter with a leak (leek) in it!"

63 He reminded me of the wife's mother—short and fat and with a big moustache . . .

My mother-in-law! . . . what a man! When I told her I wanted to marry
64 her daughter, she said, "How dare you! You marry my daughter! You're effeminate!" Me—effeminate! Mind you, next to her, I am . . . (*See pages 1–2 for detailed analysis of this gag.*)

65 Still, I do my best—I bought her a chair for her birthday. Bought her a chair . . . but the wife wouldn't let me plug it in . . .

And she's so fat! Dear oh dear—do you know, when her husband, my
66 father-in-law, married her, he told me that when the time came for him to carry her over the threshold, he had to make three trips!
(*During the laugh you can extend it by miming the carrying over of three lumps of mother-in-law, boggling all imaginations.*)

Last year she tried going on a diet; for six months all she ate was coconut
67 milk and bananas. Coconut milk and bananas for six months! (*Pause.*) She didn't lose any weight . . . but she couldn't half climb trees!

But we did have a shocking time with her once. She broke her leg in three
68 places—and I was always telling her not to go into those places. Anyway, we had to have her stay with us, of course. Had her leg in plaster, couldn't walk upstairs—for three months! And the racket she made climbing up the
69 drainpipe at bedtime . . .
(*On the tag put your hand wearily to your brow as though the racket always gave you a headache.*)

70 Then there was the time she fell asleep in the bath with the taps running. Didn't make any mess though . . . she sleeps with her mouth open.

But one night—I'll never forget!—at about three in the morning she woke us all up, shouting and screaming! The wife and I rushed into her bedroom, saying, "What's the matter?" She just kept yelling, "Get the doctor! I must

have the doctor!" We couldn't get any sense out of her, so I rang the 71
doctor. He answered and I said, "Oh, Doctor, I'm sorry to disturb you at
this time of night." He said, "That's all right, I had to get up anyway to
answer the phone. (*Wait for a good laugh here.*) What's the trouble?"

I said, "I don't know—it's the wife's mother, she just keeps shouting for
you. She won't tell us what's the matter." He said, "All right, I'll be over."

Well, he arrived and went straight up to her room. The wife and I
waited half an hour, an hour, hour and a half—he didn't come out! I said
to the wife, "We'd better go up—perhaps he needs help. Perhaps he's had 72
to give her the kiss of life and he's passed out." So she said, "No, don't go
in—just listen outside the door."

So I went up and put my ear to the keyhole—and what do you think I
heard?! "Kiss me, Doctor! Oh, kiss me!" The wife's mother! To the
doctor!!! He was very good with her, though; he handled her very well. 73
He said, "Now then, madam, that would be very unethical. You know I
mustn't do that; after all, you are my patient." He said, "Strictly speaking,
I shouldn't even be in bed with you."

But then you have to make allowances. After all, she's had twenty children. 74
Twenty kids! She must be stork raving mad . . .

So you can imagine the next day I was feeling a bit jaded, so I went into a
pub to change my breath, and I met a pal I hadn't seen for some time. 75
"Hello, Tom," I said, "you're looking well." He said, "Well, I've just got
married." I said, "That's good." He said, "Not too good—she's very
ugly." I said, "Oh, that's bad." He said, "Not too bad—she's very rich."
I said, "Oh, that's good." He said, "Not too good—she's very mean." I 76
said, "Oh, that's bad." He said, "Not too bad—we live in a lovely house."
I said, "Oh, that's good." He said, "Not too good—it burned down last
week." I said, "Oh, that's bad." He said, "Not too bad—she was in it!"
(*This last gag should be delivered speedily and very precisely; it should be
practised assiduously. Tom's lines should be delivered with a smile on the
"good" items, and a frown on the "bad" ones. Pause after each of his replies
—but only briefly—so that your audience can catch up on the plot.*)

TEN-MINUTE PATTER ACT—TWO

77 Hasn't it been marvellous, lately? The wife and I went down to the seaside last weekend, down to Brighton, I went in the sea, but it didn't come up to my expectations . . . that's the trouble with being so tall! (*or*) . . . the tide was out.
(*The laugh is really on the word "expectations", with either of the alternative following lines producing a subsiding laugh or a link with the next gag.*)

78 But the wife—her bathing costume! Really, she did embarrass me. Well—it had a hole in it! I tell you, I was so embarr—I didn't know where to put myself . . . well, you could distinctly see her left knee-cap. It was one of **79** those nuclear bathing-costumes all the girls are wearing these days—you know, lots of fall-out. (*Pick out "nuclear".*)

80 But she's a cracker the wife, she really is. She's got everything a man could desire:—big . . . biceps and a black bushy beard. (*The pause after "big" is slight but critical; a non-committal mime with the hands on "big" also helps.*) She's got big eyes, too—like saucers. And you should see her **81** cups . . .

But I was telling you about last weekend in Brighton; well, the wife sent me to get an ice-cream—it was very hot, wasn't it?—and I was standing in the queue when I saw that in front of me, in the queue, was this beautiful young girl—gorgeous figure!—and wearing the sauciest little skirt you ever saw.
(*From "I was standing in the queue" you can slow down considerably and become very quiet—a technique which many comics use, often puncturing the atmosphere they have created by saying, "hasn't it gone quiet?"*) So I was **82** bending down doing up my shoelace . . . (*this to be speeded up and said over-casually*) when she saw me and she said, "You're no gentleman." I said, "I can see you're not."

One nice thing about the hot weather is that I occasionally get a booking at a nudist camp. I did one a few weeks ago—very nice people they were **83** there. Oh, very nice. At the start of the show the band played the National Anthem; everyone stood up—when they sat down again it sounded like a round of applause . . . very encouraging . . .
(*"Very encouraging" is of course just a fill-up.*)

But a pal of mine went home one day unexpectedly and found a nude man **84** in his bedroom with his wife. She said, "Now don't get excited! (*Pause.*)

He's a nudist come in to use the phone."
(*After the laugh you can say "and he believed her . . . I dunno . . ."*)

Talking of nudes, did you hear about the gamekeeper? He was going on 85
his rounds in the woods . . . wait for it . . . when he came upon this luscious
blonde lying in the grass stark naked. She said to him, "Who are you?"
He said, "I'm the gamekeeper." She said, "Well, I'm game"—so he shot
her!
(*There can be an appreciable pause after "I'm the gamekeeper"; the rest of
the gag to be rapped out smartly.*)

I won't say she'd been a bad girl but they buried her in a Y-shaped 86
coffin . . .

But anyway, we shan't go to Brighton again—my kid made a sandcastle
on the beach. Ten minutes later a feller came up and gave me a rates 87
demand . . .

But we love wild animals, the wife and me—well, you have to, living in
(*name local rough district*) so I took her off to the zoo for a treat the other
Sunday. But when we got inside the monkey house there wasn't a monkey 88
to be seen! The wife was so upset—she said to the keeper, "Where are all
the monkeys then? I especially wanted to see them." The keeper said,
"Oh," he said, "it's the mating season, love. They're all in their little
bedroms at the back . . . mating." She said, "Oh dear, I'm so dis-
appointed." She said, "D'you think if I threw some nuts in the cage they'd 89
come out?" He said, "Well, *I* wouldn't, missus—would you?"

But she was upset. I said, "Never mind, love, when we get home I'll take 90
you round to see your mother." Her mother!!! I'll never forget the day I
first met her—God knows, I've tried. And what a terrible cook—her
daughter takes after her there . . . (*clutch your stomach and suppress the
merest suggestion of a belch*). I won't say her pastry's heavy but she's the
only woman in the street with a bow-legged gas-stove.

Mind you, she comes from a very aristocratic family. Oh yes—her grand- 91
father was a peer. Her grandmother had kidney trouble as well . . .
(*Give an appreciable pause after "peer" then throw away the tag-line. "Peer"
needs to be picked out cleanly and positively. This gag can also be used for
yourself.*)

Woman are funny though, aren't they? Did you hear about the girl who 92
went to the doctor? She said, "Doctor, I've got a very unusual complaint."
He said (*in a bored, superior tone*), "Oh yes—what's that then?" She said,
"Well, every time I sneeze . . . (*take this slowly*) . . . I get an uncontrollable
urge to make love." (*Pause while this sinks in.*) He said, "That is unusual.
Every time you sneeze you get an uncontrollable sexual urge to make
love?" She said, "Yes." He said, "How long have you had this?" She

said, "Six months." (*Another pause.*) He said, "Six months! What have you been doing about it?" She said, "Taking snuff!"
(*After the final pause take the rest swiftly.*)

93 But I went to the doctor's the other day with laryngitis. His receptionist opened the door—lovely girl—and I said (*in a whisper*), "Is the doctor here?" She said (*also in a whisper*), "No—come in!"

94 Mind you, some girls positively shrink from making love. Others get bigger and bigger.

95 There was one girl for instance got a new job. As a secretary. Very attractive—and efficient she was, too. Oh yes. Soon she was doing very well with the firm, and after six months the boss's son, he was nuts about her, he gave her a mink coat. Didn't do her much good though—after nine months she couldn't do it up.
("*Nine*" *needs to be slightly accentuated to make the point.*)

96 But there it is . . . the other day I went into a shop for some writing-paper and envelopes. I said to the girl behind the counter, "Do you keep stationery?" She said, "No, I wriggle a bit!"
(*After "stationery" crack in with the tag-line before the audience gets ahead of you. With some gags this doesn't matter—in fact it can be a positive advantage—but it's death with this particular one.*)

97 I once had a girl-friend I was very fond of, though. I gave her a watch for her birthday, and she was so pleased—she gave me a big kiss, wound up the watch, put it to her ear and said, "But, darling—it doesn't go." I said, "That's all right, I'll give you the works tomorrow . . ."
(*A contrast should be made here between the soft, gentle, sentimental delivery of the gag up to the tag, which should be lifted sharply.*)

98 The first time I met her she was a window-dresser . . . never pulled the blinds down. But she'd been married, as a matter of fact. Yes, she'd been
99 married to a trapeze artist, but she caught him in the act . . . very sad . . .
(*Pause after "trapeze artist"; "very sad" is a fill-up.*)

100 But she was a well-endowed girl—what?! I'll say! She went into a lingerie shop and said to the manager, "Have you got anything to give me a bit of uplift?" He said, "What about a fork-lift truck?"
(*Don't waste time on this one—it's just a chuckle in the general routine.*)

101 Not like the wife—a lovely girl, as I said, but flat as a pancake. I think her living bra must have died of malnutrition.

102 She was mithering on one day—you know how women do go on sometimes—she was doing the ironing and carrying on about all the housework she had to do. I said, "Well, you needn't iron that bra for a start—you've

got nothing to put in it." (*Pause for small laugh.*) She said, "Well, I iron your underpants, don't I?"

But did you hear about the new bra called "Cowboy"? It rounds 'em up **103** and heads 'em out!
(*The tag to be spoken in broad Wild West cowboy accent. Use a low register.*)

But of course I've been interested in women's clothes for years . . . on and **104** off . . . Still, I'm crazy about the wife, really. I'm only joking. I've been crazy about her since the very first day I met her. The next day we met **105** and I said to her, I said, "I dreamed about you last night." She said, "Did you?" I said, "No, you wouldn't let me."
(*Again there can be a contrast between the romantic style of delivery of this gag up to the whiplash tag-line.*)

No, well, I agree with that. All this permissiveness—there's too much of **106** it. A pal of mine said to me the other day, "I never had improper relations with my wife before we were married. Did you?" I said, "I dunno—what was her maiden name?"

Mind you, some men are very jealous. There was a chap waiting for me at **107** the stage door tonight as I came in. He said (*very angrily*), "Here—did you sleep with my wife last night?" I said (*with righteous indignation*), "No! (*Pause, but only slight*). Not a wink!"

Not like the wife of a pal of mine. He's a young businessman in Cleethorpes **108** (*or local*) and he had to give a talk to the local Chamber of Commerce. So he said to me, "What on earth can I talk about?" I said, "Sex. Everyone always likes a talk about that—go on, you tell 'em about sex." So he did, and very successful he was, too—went a bomb; they loved him. Marvellous. But when he got home and his wife asked him all about it, he was a bit embarrassed to tell her the subject he'd chosen—they hadn't been married long and besides she came from Deptford (*or local*) and you know they're a bit strait-laced there—so he said, "Oh . . . yachting." She said, "Yachting? What do you know about yachting?" He said, "Oh enough . . ." Well, next morning, the wife had to go to the bank and there she bumped into the bank manager who'd been at this meeting the night before. He said, "Your husband was very good last night. Very funny—my word!" She said, "Yes, I can't understand it—he's only tried it twice . . . the first time he was sick. The second time his hat blew off!"
(*You can take plenty of time over this gag, since the story line is comparatively complicated. There is a big laugh on "the first time he was sick" so don't lose the even bigger laugh on "the second time his hat blew off!"*)

109 But hasn't it been chilly lately, eh? Perishing . . . d'you know, on the way here I passed three brass monkeys looking distinctly worried . . .
(*It may be surprising, but this quip gets a very respectable laugh.*)

And I got frozen waiting at the bus stop—I was there for ages. I said to
110 the Inspector, "How long will the next bus be?" He said, "About twenty-four foot six." That was a lot of help, wasn't it? But when the bus did arrive, I got on board and said to the conductor, "My word, it's cold—
111 my feet are like ice." He said (*broad West Indian accent*), "Yes, man, and mine are like choc ice . . ."
(*This gag is especially popular with coloured people, so don't be afraid of offending anybody's sensibilities.*)

112 He was an Irishman . . . (*pause*) . . . you could tell he was Irish by the shamrock in his turban.

I hadn't been on the bus five minutes, it was very crowded, when this lovely, dewy-eyed young thing asks me if she could have my seat, because . . . (*look to right and left and speak conspiratorially*) . . . because she was
113 expecting. (*Continue in normal voice.*) Of course, I jumped up, she sat down, and I said, "My goodness, what a lovely creature you are"—I believe in speaking my mind, you see—"your husband must be very pleased." She said, "Yes, he is." I said, "Forgive me for saying so, but you don't look pregnant." She said, "Well, it's only been half an hour but doesn't it make your back ache?"

Then there was a spot of bother at a stop. A chap tried to get on with this enormous great big dog. The conductor said, (*using the same West*
114 *Indian accent*), "You can't come on my bus with that dog." The feller said, "Oh, go on, he's very quiet—he'll be no bother." The conductor said, "No, he's much too big. You can't come on my bus with that dog." So the chap said, "Well, you know what you can do with your bus!" And the conductor said, "Well, if you can do the same with your dog you can come on my bus . . ."
(*The dog-owner's angry last line should be contrasted by the air of sweet reason evinced by the conductor in his last line.*)

Then a few people got off so I went upstairs to have a smoke—I smoke a
115 pipe, myself. Oh yes, I love a good shag. Anyway, there was this young couple in the back seat—only kids they were, really—locked in a passionate embrace. Do you know, he kissed her all the way from the top of

Primrose Hill (*or local*) . . . right down to Hampstead Pond (*or local*)! Eventually they pulled apart (*making pop sound with finger in cheek*), and sat gazing into each other's eyes, breathing hard. Then the girl said (*panting*), "Here, Engelbert . . . (*or currently fashionable name such as Jason or Jeremy; the girl should also speak in a broad regional accent*) . . . **116** got any fags?" The boy was so upset, he said, "Have I——? Ain't yer got no finer feelings? Ain't yer got no emotions?" (*Slight pause.*) She said, "I dunno—but I know I ain't got any fags . . ."

Of course, I'd love to have a car, but they're so expensive to run these **117** days, aren't they? I got rid of my old banger last month. No, I don't mean I got a divorce . . . I got rid of my old car—swopped it for a bike and a second-hand jockstrap. You know what a jockstrap is, don't you? . . . a Scotsman's mouth . . .   **118**
(*Don't wait after "second-hand jockstrap".*)

But it's so dangerous on the roads nowadays. There were these two country farmlads driving a cartload of . . . stuff, along a country lane. They were doing about three and a half miles an hour, blocking the entire **119** road—they'd just pulled out of a field—when a brand-new supercharged Jag came roaring round a bend right at them! The driver had no time to stop, he swerved off the road, into the field and smashed right into an old oak tree. One of the farmlads turned to the other and said, "Hey, Tom— we just got out o' that field in toime . . .!"
(*This can also be set in Ireland to advantage. The drama can be heightened by speeding up your delivery on the penultimate sentence. Then there can be an appreciable pause, and a strong contrast gained by having the tag spoken slowly.*)

But it is cold, though—I must get Granny's legs lagged.   **120**

She's a funny old stick, my Granny. Doesn't matter how cold it is, she will go out and get the coal in her nightie. Last winter I bought her a **121** shovel but she said her nightie holds more.
(*Pause after "get the coal in her nightie" to let this sink in well.*)

And of course you feel so ill with this weather, don't you? As a matter of **122** fact the wife was going to come along tonight but she told me this morning when she woke up she was feeling a little dicky . . . I said, "Sorry, love, I never noticed"—well, I said it was cold—and she was so upset! She burst into tears and said, "You never notice anything! You don't love me any more!" What can you say? I said, "Of course I do, darling, I do, I do, I do!" She said, "Well, why are you always going down that pub, then? **123** You know what it does to the sheets . . . why are you always leaving me in alone night after night? I know what it is," she said. "It's that brassy barmaid at the Knacker's. Yes, it is! It's that brassy barmaid. What's she got that I haven't got?" (*Pause.*) I said, "Some clean glasses and a good pair of pumps!"   **124**

D

(The wife's dialogue will need to be delivered tearfully at first, changing to indignation.)

But she's always moaning—after all, I did take her out last Christmas. We went into Town to a posh place for a bit of a change. I went up and said to
125 the fellow behind the bar, "Do you serve ladies here?" He said, "No—you have to bring your own." But it was very posh. At the table next to us there was this foursome, two couples. One of the husbands—he'd had a few—he belched good and loud. The other chap was furious, he said,
125a "How dare you belch before my wife!" He said *(drunkenly)*, "I'm terribly sorry—I didn't know it was her turn!"
("Last Christmas" should be altered, if you are performing in the New Year, to "last Easter"; if at Easter make it "last summer", etc.)

Then a funny thing happened—a little boy of about ten came in and sat
126 down at one of the tables, all by himself. A waitress came over, he said, "Bring us a double Scotch!" She said, "I can't do that—you're under age." He said, "I don't care about that—bring us a double Scotch. Neat!" She said, "I've told you, I can't—you're under age. Do you want to get me into trouble?" He said, "Never mind the sex—just bring me my double Scotch!"
(The tag must follow quickly after "Do you want to get me into trouble?")

127 By the way, we're offering a free drink to everyone here tonight. Yes, a free drink with every fifty pence packet of crisps . . .
(Or "a free cup of tea" if there is only a snack bar.)

Then on the wife's birthday I took her to a concert at the Albert Hall. Another freezing cold night it was—no tubes, they'd packed up—couldn't get a bus or taxi because of the fog—so we had to walk. Neither of us had been there before, we weren't sure of the way, but just off the Cromwell Road I spotted this chap with a violin case under his arm, so I said, "Can
128 you tell me how to get to the Albert Hall?" He said, "Practice, my boy—years of practice!"
(After the tag you can do a little mime of earnest violin playing.)

129 Mind you, my sister used to be a musician. At least I think she must have been a violinist because I remember her asking me one day if I'd seen her G-string . . . all right, I'm only kidding—I know she was a stripper. She
129a had a marvellous figure, though—all she used to wear was three beads . . . and two of them were sweat. But one day she retired—she couldn't bear it any longer. Where was I? Oh, yes . . .

130 Anyhow, the missus and I eventually reached the Albert Hall. Well, I said it was a terrible night and—do you know?—we were the only two people to turn up. The place was empty—not a soul! You'd have thought Dorothy Squires was appearing . . . the manager came over to us and said the concert would be cancelled. I was choked, I can tell you! I went

straight round to Yehudi's dressing-room—yes, he was top of the bill—
and said, "Now look here, Mr Menuhin, the wife and me have walked
all the way in this shocking weather to hear you and now the concert's
cancelled. I think you might at least give us one song!" And he did!!
There and then—in his dressing-room . . . and then I understood why the
wife and me were the only ones to turn up. Of course, he used to be an
organist, you know, but someone shot his monkey.
(*The reference to Dorothy Squires can be altered to suit a local audience.*)

But you know that old saying, "Music hath charms to soothe the savage **131**
beast"? Here was this old boy who decided to try and prove it. He took
his fiddle into the heart of the African jungle, miles from anywhere, and
started to play in this clearing in the bush. Well, the birds stopped chirping
and sat silent in their trees, the monkeys stopped howling and came to
have a listen, the lions stopped roaring and padded into the clearing. The
elephants came, and the giraffes and the hippos—all the animals and birds
and insects for miles around gathered to hear this old chap play. They all **132**
sat round entranced by his fiddling—he used to be a stockbroker—when
an old crocodile came lumbering up out of the river, through the trees,
into the clearing, up to the old chap, opened its jaws, and—snap!—gobbled
him up in one bite! The animals were furious, and one of the lions said to
the crocodile, "What did you have to go and do a thing like that for? We
were enjoying that." And the crocodile said (*cupping one hand to ear*),
"Eh?"

But that's show business; you meet some funny people. Actually, I've just **133**
done a split week at the Hippodrome, Land's End, and the Coliseum,
John o' Groats. I got to the Hippodrome on the Monday, I said to the
stage-manager, "What are they like here, then?" He said, "Well, we had
Samson here last week!" "Oh?" I said, "did they like him?" "Like him?" **134**
he said, "—he brought the house down!"
(*The stage-manager needs to have a "Doctor Cameron" accent; the tag
wants to be delivered very swiftly and lightly—almost as an afterthought.*)

Then the week before I played a tiny date—the Abattoir, Aberystwyth. I **135**
really slayed 'em . . . It's nice back-stage there, though—running-water on
every floor. Mind you, it makes the dog-ends soggy . . . And my dressing-
room was small—every time I stood up I hit my head on this chain . . .
(*These gags are just quips to make a break between the longer stories, so
don't lean on them too much.*)

But talking of theatres, I understand some of you are a little worried about
the fire precautions here. Well, I've been asked to tell you that you need
have absolutely no cause for alarm, and to illustrate the point, I'd like to
tell you a story of the great opera house in Milan, where on Saturday
night, when it was packed to the rafters, the dread cry of "Fire!" rang out. **136**
Immediately there was a terrible panic—the place was full of Italians, you

see—and there was pandemonium as everyone began pushing and shoving their way to the exits.

Well, people were getting trampled underfoot, when the leading tenor, with great presence of mind, stepped forward and began to sing—he was a visiting English tenor, as it happened. . . . And as his glorious, mellifluous tones—that's a nice word, isn't it? I'll say it again. And as his glorious, mellifluous tones soared out through that vast auditorium, the panic began to subside and everyone settled back in their seats. And do you know, ladies and gentlemen, every single person in that opera house was —burned to a cinder.

(Before "burned to a cinder" there needs to be a fractional pause. Tell this story slowly and deliberately.)

137 But you can't be too careful. A pal of mine moved into a new house a couple of weeks ago and invited me round to have a look at it. Very nice place—he showed me into the living-room. "Double-glazing at the front," he said proudly, "fully centrally heated." Then he went to the french windows at the back, opened them, looked out and called, "Green side up." *(Pause while you look blank.)* Then we went upstairs to the bathroom. Very nice—tiles all round, low-flush, footbath—smashing. He opened the window, looked down and called out, "Green side up." *(Again pause as you think about this, puzzled.)* He took me into the bedroom—lovely! Fitted cupboards, mirrors all over the ceiling—super! Again he opened the window, looked down and called out, "Green side up!" I said to him, "Look, Evelyn"—he was a funny sort of bloke—"look, Evelyn, it's a smashing house, but why do you keep looking out the back and calling 'green side up'?" He said, "Oh, that's the garden—I've got a couple of Irishmen laying the lawn . . ."

(You can also take your time with this one, since the tag is never anticipated, and the story presents an intriguing mystery.)

TWELVE-MINUTE PATTER ACT

Hello—I'm only here because I'm out of work. You don't think I'd do this for a living, do you? Oh no . . . if my old professor could see me now, he'd turn in his gymslip . . . (*after laugh*) . . . there's a lot of it about. **138** (*Look at rear of auditorium.*) Never mind, Harry . . . (*or whatever is the name of the manager*) . . . they can't touch you for it . . . no, but he's a boy, old Harry, he's a boy . . . at least I hope he is . . . all this Women's Lib you hear about so much nowadays, though—I don't know whether **139** it's the emancipation of women or the enancipation of men!

But he's so mean—he's the only man I know with an ingrown wallet. The **140** money here's terrible—I tell you, if this was China, I'd be picketed by coolies . . . still, you get a nice tan from the lights. **141**

But I see in the (*local newspaper*) that the police in (*local area*) are looking for a tall, handsome man for assaulting women . . . I thought if the money **142** was good I might apply.
(*Alter the physical description to match your own; don't allow too long a pause after "assaulting women" or you may be anticipated.*)

Well, I've just lost my job, you see. I was working as a Corporation dustman—dustman! Ten quid a week and as much as you can eat . . . well, **143** you have to do something, don't you?

But I met a pal the other day I knew had been out of work. I said to him, "Any luck, then?" He said, "Yeah—got a smashing job!" I said, "That's good. What are you doing then?" He said, "I'm working in the circus—mucking out the elephants!" I said, "Mucking out the elephants! How many are there?" He said, "Fifteen!" I said, "That sounds like heavy **144** work . . . how much do they pay you, then?" He said, "Eight quid a week and my keep." I said, "Eight quid and ——! Why don't you chuck it and get a decent job?" He said, "What—and give up show business?"
(*There are more laughs here than may be apparent, so pause for them after "mucking out the elephants", "fifteen!", and "that sounds like heavy work". The tag should be said in tones of lofty disdain.*)

But my old man had a funny job once—he was a traveller in Beecham's **145** Pills . . . his area was Russia. Yes—Russia! No—he did well at it . . . after all, they were always having purges in Russia . . . did you know in Russia they've got a standing army of 30,000 men? (*Slight pause.*) They're very short of chairs in Russia . . . **146**

(*Pause after "Beecham's Pills" and the first mention of Russia to let this rather bizarre information sink in.*)

147 But he had a very distinguished service career, in the Army. Oh yes,—he fought with Mountbatten in Burma, with Alexander in Tunis, with Monty at Alamein . . . he couldn't get on with anybody . . . (*this is a throwaway tag, but a good laugh.*)

148 But I've been in the Army myself, you know. Did my National Service— oh yes. For two years I wore Her Majesty's uniform . . . 'course, it fitted her better . . . but I come from an old military family—one of my ancestors
149 fell at Waterloo . . . someone pushed him off platform nine . . . (*Allow only the slightest pause after "Her Majesty's uniform", also after "fell at Waterloo". Both these very obvious gags are solid buffs—perhaps because they are so obvious.*)

150 But I'm the last of my line . . . apart from a sister in the Tank Corps . . .

151 Mind you, the theatre's in my blood, too. I was born in the theatre, you know. Oh yes . . . it went over so big my mother kept it in the act . . . (*Make the tag a fast throw-away.*)

152 But I had a great time in the Army. I was ADC to a general . . . ADC, that's Ada Camp . . . and I was lucky enough to travel a good deal— Singapore, Samarkand, the Yemen . . . Shepton Mallet . . . In Australia I
153 tried surf riding, but I couldn't get the horse near the water . . .

154 No, I had a great time—I remember when we were in India a new officer came to join the regiment. The Colonel said to him, "Welcome to the regiment, Strap . . ." (*the audience is waiting for a pay-off, so add, as an afterthought*): You've probably heard of his brother, Jock . . . (*believe me when I say that this is a yock*). The Colonel said, "You must understand that we need a very special type of officer out here. I need support from my officers, Strap, so we need a man who is courageous and resourceful. Therefore we have a little test that we ask all newcomers to the mess to undergo, to see if you're really suited to this posting." He said, "Certainly, sir. Anything you say, sir!" (*This said saluting wildly.*)
The Colonel said, "The test is quite simple. It's in two parts. First of all you have to go down into the village market-place, take the first woman you see, rip off her veil, and kiss her full on the lips." Now this is much more dangerous than you might think, because the men there are very jealous, and they carry these wicked-looking long curved knives—they can inflict a lot of damage very easily (*wince at the thought as you subtly suggest castration by a non-committal gesture*). Then the Colonel said, "The second part of the test is that you must go straight into the jungle, and the first tiger you see you must shoot dead right between the eyes with one shot. Understand?" (*Saluting again.*) "Yes, sir. Certainly, sir. Understood, sir." With that the Colonel gave him a rifle with one round up the spout

. . . (*"up the spout" sometimes gets a chuckle*) and away went Captain
Strap.
  About a week later the Colonel heard a tap on his door. He said,
"Come in!" The door opened, and there, battered, bleeding, his uniform
in ribbons, was Strap! He crawled along the floor, heaved himself up to
his feet, saluted (*suit the action to the word*) and said: "Right, sir! Where's
this woman I've got to shoot between the eyes?!"
(*The tag must be said gasping as though in extremis. After "come in!" you
can take this quite deliberately, since the audience will be enthralled to know
how the bold Captain has fared.*)

  Once I was sent to Moscow—I was military attaché at the embassy . . . I
carried the cases . . . well, I didn't fancy that as a posting after the girls in
the Orient, I can tell you. I thought to myself, I thought, "All those great,
square, lady tractor-drivers with a mouthful of steel teeth . . . oh dear, oh
dear . . . but anyway, at the very first official dinner I attended I was sat
next to the most luscious, gorgeous beauty I'd ever clapped eyes on!
(*Dwell on the girl's charms.*)   **155**
  She didn't say much but she seemed friendly enough, so as we started
the soup I dropped my napkin, bent down to pick it up and put my hand
on her ankle . . . I looked up and she was smiling at me! A bit later I
dropped my place card—oh yes, it was a posh do, not a chip or a sauce
bottle in sight—I dropped my place card, bent down to pick it up—and
put my hand on her knee! (*Pause for the audience to savour what might
follow.*) I looked up and she was grinning openly.
  Then a bit later I saw her writing on her place card, so I thought to
myself, "Hello, here we go! She's been around, she knows the drill. Place,
date, time—this is it!" Then she passed the card along to me under the
table and I read: "Mind how you go. Signed, Carruthers—MI5."
(*On the tag mime reading a card held under the table; keep your eyes down
as you "read" and hold the pose for the laugh.*)

  No luck at all—like a pal of mine. He'd been married a few weeks, I met
him in the street so I said, "How's married life, then?". . . not very original,
but friendly. He said, "Not so good. It's the wife—she's frigid, completely
frigid!" I said, "What—not once?" (*Pause for the implication to sink in.*) **156**
He said, "Not once!" I said, "But that's terrible! What are you going to
do about it?" He said, "Well, I've just been to see the doctor, and he said
there's nothing wrong with her really. It's just her nerves." He said, "He's
advised me to grab her and make love to her when she's least expecting it.
Then once she realises it's not so bad we should be all right."
  I met him again a month or two later. I said. "How's things, then?" He
said, "Great!" I said, "Oh, good—you took the doctor's advice, then?"
He said, "Yes, and it worked a treat!" I said, "That's marvellous. How
did you manage it?" He said, "Well, we were having tea one day, and I
thought to myself, 'she'll never expect me to have a go at her now' so I
said to her, 'pass the jam, love', and as she passed the jam, I grabbed her
wrist, swept everything on to the floor, and made love to her there and

then . . . on the table . . . since then everything's been fine. (*Pause*.) Mind
you—we can't eat in Lyons' any more . . ." (*Tell this one swiftly*.)

157 But I still like old Joe Lyons', don't you? I especially like their three-
course dinners—two chips and a pea.

158 But men do funny things for love, don't they? Like Van Gogh—you
know, the artist chap Van Gogh. You know what he did? He cut his ear
off—cut his ear off! He packed it up in a box and posted it off to his girl
friend as a token of his love. Well, she was tickled pink—no one had ever
cut a bit of himself off for her before—so the next time she saw him she
gave him a big kiss and said, "Oh, thanks ever so much for the ear." She
said, "What a wonderful thing to do to show me how much you love me
. . . but tell me," she said, "when you cut it off—didn't it hurt?" And he
said (*cupping hand to ear*), "Eh?"
(*As I have already said, you must enunciate the two mentions of the word
"ear" very clearly*.)

159 But I used to do a bit of the old portrait-painting, you know. Oh yes—
one day a lovely girl came to see me and said, "Can you paint me in the
nude?" I said, "Certainly, madam, as long as I can keep my socks on—I
must have somewhere to put the brushes . . ."
(*Speak the last line rapidly and without pause*.)

160 But it's something to do, it keeps you from thinking about yourself too
much. Otherwise you can get very lonely, can't you? A fellow I knew,
once, he suffered terribly from loneliness so the doctor advised him to get
a pet for company. He said, "What kind of pet?" The doctor said, "Well,
why not get a talking bird? That'll be company for you." So he did, he
went to a pet shop and asked the chap behind the counter for a talking
budgie. The man showed him one, he said, "Is he a good talker?"
The man said, "Oh, yes, a wonderful talker. Rabbits on all the time."
So he said, "Right—how much?" The feller said, "Five pounds."
(*Pause*.)
   He said, "Five pounds! That's very expensive, isn't it?" The feller said,
"Well, he is a very good talker, sir." So he said, "All right, then, I'll take
him." And home he went with the budgie in his cage—that cost him another
tenner.
   Well, that afternoon, that evening, next morning—the budgie still
hadn't spoken, so he went back to the shop and complained. The feller
behind the counter said, "I can't understand it, sir." He said, "He seems
quite happy, does he? Looking all perky? Swinging on his perch?"
(*Slight pause*.) The chap said, "Perch? What perch?" The feller said, "Oh,
well, there's your trouble—he must have a perch." (*Reach down and lift up
an imaginary perch which you place on an imaginary counter*.) "Here you
are, sir. One budgie perch. Fifty pence."
   So home he went, put the perch in the cage, but still nary a syllable out
of the budgie—not a twitter! Next day he was back at the shop: "It's still

not talking—that budgie you sold me." The feller said, "That's odd . . . looks quite perky, does he? Swinging on his perch? Ringing his bell. . .?" (*Slightly longer pause.*) "Bell—what bell?" "Oh, well, he must have a bell. Here you are—(*again reaching down and placing on counter*) one budgie bell. Fifty pence." He took the bell, and away he went.

Next day he was back again! "That budgie's still not talking to me!" "I can't make it out, sir . . . he's looking perky, is he? Swinging on his perch?" "Yes." "Ringing his bell?" "Yes." "Running up and down his ladder. . .?"

(*This mention of yet another toy stops the fast interchange very suddenly —the two men can be indicated by slight changes in the direction you are facing. After "running up and down his ladder . . .", as I have said, stop abruptly, pause, then look chagrined and slowly mime reaching for money —only an indication is needed: the mime needn't be carried through.*)

The next day it was a mirror, the day after that a plastic budgie for company, until that cage was jam-packed with toys and ornaments and what-have-you. And *still* . . . not a single . . . solitary . . . word. After two weeks of this, the chap came running into the pet shop, he said (*puffed and distraught*), "That budgie you sold me—he's dead!" (*Pause for reaction.*) The man behind the counter said, "Oh, I'm terribly sorry to hear that, sir. What a shame. But tell me," he said. "Did he never say anything at all?" He said, "Yes, he did . . . just before he died. (*Pause—they will all be hanging on to this.*) He said (*gather yourself and say in agonised tones*), 'Don't they sell any bloody birdseed in that shop!' "

(*This lengthy but excellent story needs to be practised, since it is technically not an easy story to tell. The danger is lack of variation of pace in a long gag, so I would suggest that the first paragraph, which is only setting-up the situation, be taken quite rapidly. Then slow down when recounting how the bird will not talk and the second scene in the pet shop. The questions put by the man behind the counter need to be all inflected exactly the same —"Swinging on his perch? Ringing his bell? etc., etc.," and the pauses after these questions get progressively longer. The final scene in the shop can be taken very quickly, apart from the indicated pause after "he's dead!", until the poor budgie's dying speech, which will be well pointed up.*)

Here—did you hear about the new tomcat that arrived in the neighbourhood? All the lady cats were discussing him and one said, "Don't waste your time on him, girls—all he talks about is his operation . . ." 161

But I like the story of the two honeymoon couples who arrived at the same 162 hotel at the same time. The wives went upstairs and the husbands stayed down in the bar for a couple of jars; then they both went up at the same time. As they got on the landing outside their rooms the fuses went, and in the ensuing confusion the wrong husband went into the wrong room with the wrong wife. Well, one of them was very religious, so after he'd got undressed—didn't take long—he knelt down by the side of the bed to say his prayers. As he finished the lights came on again; he glanced up, saw it wasn't his wife in the bed, realised what had happened, jumped up,

ran across the room, pulled open the door, dashed into the other bedroom
—and found the other chap was an atheist . . .
(*After "realised what had happened" take it very fast until "dashed into the
other bedroom" at which point come to a dead stop, and say the tag very
matter-of-factly.*)

163 'Course, I'm married myself—I've got a little boy. Not that I see much of
him, I'm sorry to say. Well, in this business you have to travel so much.
In fact I see so little of him he calls me Uncle Father. But I once over-
heard him talking to the little boy next door—nice kid—and the two little
'uns were chatting. "I'se five. How old are you?" said this kid to my lad.
"Dunno," said my kid—he's like his mother; stupid. So the other kid
164 said, "Do girls bother you?" And my kid said, "No." (*Pause.*) So he
said, "You'se four . . ."

165 We had a rough time at home lately, though. The wife had a toothache—
but she would not go to the dentist . . . she's so frightened of them.
Eventually I couldn't stand it any longer, so I made the appointment and
dragged her along. As she sat in his chair, she said, "Oh, I'm so scared
of dentists! I don't know which is worse—seeing the dentist or having a
baby." He said, "Well, make up your mind before I adjust the chair."
(*Speak the tag quickly after "having a baby".*)

166 But I've not been so hot, either—my housemaid's knee has been giving
me trouble . . . the wife caught me sitting on it . . .

167 But I was working with a chap last summer in a shocking state. I said to
him, "What's the trouble with you, then?" He said, "Well . . . I've got . . .
boils on my botty." I said, "That's nasty! Why don't you go to the doctor,
then?" He said, "I don't like to—I'm embarrassed." I said, "Look, I'll tell
you what to do—when I was a kid and we had boils my old Mum used to
put tea-leaves on 'em. That always did the trick—why don't you try that?"
He said, "Thanks, I will." Well, he was a bit thick, this feller, and he
brewed up some tea and slapped the tea-leaves on his . . . infected area . . .
168 without letting 'em get cold first! So now of course he was in agony, what
with burnt boils on his botty . . . so he *had* to see the doctor. It was an
Indian doctor as it happened, and when my pal dropped his trousers to
show him what was wrong, the doctor said, "Oh dear, oh dear, oh dearic
me! Oh, my goodness gracious—oh dearie dearie me, my word!" My pal
said (*worried*), "What's the matter, Doctor? What can you see?" He said,
"What can I see? . . . I see a tall, handsome stranger . . ."
(*The doctor doesn't have to be Indian of course—in fact he can be quite
straight. Tell the start of the gag swiftly, since the story line is quite simple.
Then slow up when describing the fact of the tea-leaves being hot. The
doctor's "What can I see?" should be said with amazement, and the tag-line
intoned like a gipsy reading a tea-cup. Accentuate the alliteration on "burnt
boils on his botty".*)

RECITATION: THE PIGTAIL OF LI FANG FU
by
SAX ROHMER

I have abridged and slightly amended this remarkable poem to suit my own purposes, and can recommend it as an unusual and very funny recitation. Its humour, however, depends to a great extent on the personality and histrionic power of the executant; it is best attempted, therefore, only by comics with "straight" experience. It is especially suitable for a Chairman's solo turn in an Old Time Music Hall programme, since it fits the period style and affords a good contrast with the singers and patter comics.

I pronounce the name in the title as L-eye Fang Foo rather than Lee Fang Few since L-eye offers more opportunity for breadth, and Foo sounds more oriental.

The performer must remain completely serious throughout; any hint that he is himself aware of the absurdity of the poem will render the whole exercise sterile, besides detracting from those occasions when he is carried away by the mention of whips and blood. The opening paragraph is needed to explain the word "chandu" (shandoo) and, suitably altered, can be given by the compere if the executant is not appearing in this role himself.

*   *   *

Ladies and gentlemen, we hear a great deal nowadays about the growth of drug-addiction in our society. I would like now, therefore, to harrow you with a poem concerning this vile habit; a poem which deals with the taking of opium, or, as it is known in the East—the black chandu. Ladies and gentlemen, prepare yourselves now for an onslaught upon your finer sensibilities as I give you Mr Sax Rohmer's "The Pig-tail of Li Fang Fu".

mmmmm—They speak!
(*cough*)
   Of a dead man's vengeance;

The mmm's indicate a winding-up, rather like a tennis-player making a service. "They speak" should be very loud.

(*in a whisper*)
They whisper a deed—of hell!
'Neath the mosque of
      Mohammed Ali,
And this!—
    —is the thing they tell.

Point upwards with left forefinger.
Point upwards with right forefinger.

In a deep and midnight gully,   *This stanza to be spoken rapidly.*
By the street where the
                goldsmiths are,
'Neath the mosque of   *Point upwards with left forefinger.*
                Mohammed Ali,
At the back of the Scent   *Point over shoulder with right*
                Bazaar—   *thumb*

Lies—   *Pull up speed of delivery sharply.*
    —The House of a Hundred   *Both arms outstretched for maxi-*
                Rupt-Raptures!   *mum dramatic effect which is*
                                           ruined by that unfortunate slip of
                                           the tongue. Hold pose with hands
                                           limp while laugh lasts, looking
                                           chagrined.

The tomb of a Thousand Sighs;
Where the sleepers lay in that   *Bring up "death".*
                living death,
That the opium smoker—dies!   *Point this line very deliberately.*
                                           Drop hands hammily on "dies".

And there was a grey-haired   *Hands down by sides.*
    soldier,
The wreck of a splendid man;   *Heavy accent on "splendid".*
When the place was still,
I've heard "Mounted Drill",
Being muttered by—Captain Dan.   *Army salute on "Captain Dan",*
                                           which should be delivered with an
                                           upward inflection.

Then one night as I lay
    a-dreaming,
There were frenzied,   *Not too big on "frenzied,*
    shuddering screams;   *shuddering"—there's a long way*
                                           to go!
But the smoke cast a spell upon   *"Me" to be pronounced shortly as*
    me,   *"meh".*
I was chained to me couch of   *Both fists clenched as though*
    dreams!   *chained.*

All me strength, all me will had
    left me,
Because of the black chandu;
And there on the floor,   *Indicate with your right hand.*
By the close-barred—door,   *Tiny pause before "door" as you*
                                           realise you have indicated the
                                           wrong place on the previous line.
                                           Now you indicate with left hand.

Lay—the daughter of Li Fang
  Fu!

*Your eyes gleam with concu-
piscence.*

The daintiest ivory maiden,

*This said with a light, caressing
tone and expression.*

That ever a man called fair,
And I saw blood drip—

*The memory causes you to grimace
like Dracula about to have his
supper.*

  —where Li Fang Fu's whip,
Had tattered her shoulders bare!

*Lash to and fro with gusto.
Cross your arms and fell your own
shoulders.*

I fought for the power to curse
  him!
But never a word would come.
To reach him—
       —and to kill him!
But opium had stricken me
  dumb!

Still holding your shoulders.

*Stretch out a hand agonizedly.
Mime throttling action. Heavy
accent on "kill".
Hands drop impotently by your side.*

He lashed her again and again!

*Suddenly you thrash about
frenziedly again.*

'Till she uttered a moaning
  prayer;
And as he whipped, so the red
  blood dripped,
From those ivory shoulders bare!

*Cease your labours for "moaning"
on which you moan.
Redouble your lashing—really
enjoying yourself by now.
Slow down and stop whipping;
caress your shoulders again. After
"bare" lick your lips involuntarily.*

Then—crash—went the window
  behind me,
And in leapt a grey-haired man;
As he tore the whip
From Li Fang Fu's grip,
I knew him! 'Twas—
       —Captain Dan!

Very big on "crash".

*Suit the action to the word.
Right forefinger pointing upwards.
Right hand gives Army salute. Wait
for cheers.*

Ne'er a word spoke he, but
  remorseless, grim;
His brow with anger black;

*Gear-change here; speak this
quietly and menacingly, but swiftly
so as not to lose momentum.*

And he lashed and lashed,
  Till the shirt was slashed,

*Again you explode into action with
the whip, this time getting so
carried away with blood-lust that*

From the Chinaman's writing
  back!

And when in his grasp the whip
  broke short,
He cut with a long, keen knife—
The pigtail—for which a
  Chinaman
Would barter his soul, his life!

Yes, he cut the pigtail from Li
  Fang Fu!
And this is the thing they tell—
With it—
      —he lashed the Chinaman!

And it led to a deed of hell.

Then Li Fang Fu dropped limply
  down,
Too feeble, it seemed to stand;
But swift to arise, with blood in
  his eyes,
And the long keen knife in his
  hand!

Like fiends in an opium vision,
They closed in a fight for life;
And nearer the breast of the
  Captain crept,
The blade of the gleaming knife!

Then a shot!

        A groan!

          And a wisp of smoke!

I swooned!
        And knew no more—

*you turn right round and lose the
audience for a second.
You also writhe.*

*This is plot, so you must have
recovered a little. Hold the knife
in your right hand. Pull out your
pigtail from behind your head
with your left hand and cut it off.*

This is to be said very big.

*Quietly.
Your final chance with the whip.
Make the most of it. Then stop,
glazed and panting. Quietly with
a downward inflection: "hell" can
be in a whisper.*

Very low tones, breathing hard.

*Swiftly on an upward inflection
crescendo. Quickly on to next
stanza.*

Underline "fiends".

*Hold the knife in your right hand
and clasp your right wrist with
with the left hand to stop being
stabbed.*

*Both hands in the air with a
surprised expression.
Basso-profundo. Hands down by
sides with palms facing audience.
Right hand indicates wisp. Vocally
this should be very light as though
you were talking about a fairy.
Falsetto, even.*

*Back of right hand to brow.
Eyes shut.*

Save that Li Fang Fu lay dead!
In a red pool by the—door.

Again you indicate at first with right
hand then change to left hand.
LONG PAUSE TO COLLECT YOURSELF

'Twas the end of that long, hot
   summer
When Fate, or some wild surmise,
Drew me steps again to the gully,
To the Tomb of a Thousand
   Sighs.

Very studiedly casual.

Arms by sides.

There the door of the House lay
   open—
All the blood in me heart ran
   cold—
For within sat the golden idol,
And he leered—
   —as he leered—
      —of old.

Start building up the tension again.

Hand on heart.

Give a leer.
Do it again.
And a third time after "old".

And I thought that his eyes were
   moving,
In a sinister, vile, grimace;
When suddenly there at his feet
   I saw,
A staring and well-known face!

Make a meal of "eyes". Roll your
eyeballs on "moving".

Right hand indicates the body with
palm down.
"Face" delivered with upward
inflection.

With the shriek of a soul in
   torment,
I turned like a frenzied man!
Falling back from the spot
Where the moonlight poured
Down upon—Captain Dan.

The word "shriek" should be just
that.
Half-turn and retire.

Return gingerly, looking down.
Give a pathetic salute.

He was dead!
   And his death was fearful,
His features a—
   —ghastly hue;
For snake-like round his neck was
   wound,
The Pigtail
   of Li
      Fang
        Fu!

Drop on one knee, still looking at
body.
Look at audience.
Look at body, shudder.
"Wind" pigtail round your neck,
then cross your fists so that they
are under each ear.
Pull fists across your body as
though
frontally garrotting yourself on
"Fu"; fall flat on your face. With

*any luck your audience will say the
last line with you.*

BLACK OUT

For your calls, you will of course be overcome with emotion; shaking your
head and clutching on to the curtains, wings, etc. Having performed this
recitation many times myself I am convinced that the spectators should
feel that the performer, when lashing about with the whip, is unaware of
his own sadistic tendencies, and that they are watching a man making the
most ridiculous fool of himself without knowing it. He is exposing his own
vices while deploring them in others—a hypocritical attitude which is, or
so we are told, a characteristic of the British and one which they therefore
seem to respond to.

RECITATION: THE YARN OF THE NANCY BELL

I have performed W. S. Gilbert's famous narrative poem many times in various versions and in various ways; the following text has therefore been fired and refined in the crucible of experience and found to be strongly effective.

Introduction: And now a dramatic recitation—but not for the squeamish or the faint-hearted. If you have tears prepare to shed them now, as we present Sir William *Schwenck* Gilbert's macabre epic, entitled "The Yarn of The Nancy Bell", as rendered in truly *awful* fashion, by N——.

	Enter, stand centre and bow in dignified fashion. Start quite lightly and conversationally. On "round" indicate a circle with both hands.
'Twas on the shores that round our coast,	
From Deal to Ramsgate span;	*Indicate Deal with right hand, Ramsgate with left. Hold pose.*
That I found alone on a piece of stone,	
An elderly, naval man.	*On "naval" point to navel with left hand. On "man" stand to attention and give naval salute (with palm of right hand facing downwards).*
His hair was weedy, his beard was long,	*On "weedy" indicate long hair with both hands; on "beard" indicate long beard with right hand.*
And weedy and long was he;	*Repeat actions swiftly on "weedy" and "long".*
And I heard this wight, on the shore recite,	*On "wight" indicate with right hand to the same place as on "stone" in first stanza.*
In a singular minor key:	*On "key" mime turning key in a lock with right hand.*
"Oh, I am a cook and a captain bold,	*Assume gruff Devon accent—or any regional accent in which you feel comfortable. On "cook" mime*

E

*stirring with right hand, holding
mixing bowl in left hand. Legs
should be apart and slightly bent.
On "captain bold" straighten legs
and clasp both hands behind back.*

And the mate o' the Nancy brig;

*On "mate" mime holding telescope
to eye—pull hands down for "Nancy
brig" to ensure audibility.*

And a bos'un tight, and a
midshipmite,

*On "bos'un tight" hold fists up in
boxer's attitude; on "midshipmite",
which should be spoken in an upper-
class little boy's voice, bring feet
together and give naval salute,
looking upwards as though short in
stature.*

And the crew of the captain's
gig."

*On "crew" turn slightly sideways to
the audience and mime rowing;
keeping the rhythm to the metre,
i.e. pull oars back on "crew" and
on "gig".*

*Assume normal stance, relaxed
with hands hanging loosely by side.*

"Oh, elderly man, it's little I
know,

*On "elderly man" indicate his posi-
tion to right. On "I know" indicate
self with left hand. Stress the "I",
with a patronizing expression.*

Of the duties of men of the sea;

*On "sea" assume hornpipe pose
with back of right hand on stomach
and back of left hand in small of
back. Also go up slightly on right
toe, accentuating rising inflection.*

But I'll eat my hand if I
understand,

*On "hand" (which should be
stressed) hold up right hand by
right shoulder, palm facing front,
and point to it with left hand.*

However you can be—

*Drop both hands with palms up,
Look to wight's position right.*

At once a cook and a captain bold,
And the mate o' the Nancy brig;
And a bos'un tight, and a
midshipmite,
And the crew of the captain's
gig?"

*Movements as for third stanza.
Keep it brisk but clean cut with
slight pauses as indicated by the
punctuation. Each "and" should be
increasingly stressed so that the
last one is almost falsetto. Keep the
interrogative tone well marked.*

Then he gave a hitch to his trousers, which	*Pull trousers up with both thumbs in front of waistband; run on "trousers, which" pausing minutely after which but keep sense running on to next line. On "which" raise right index finger.*
Is a trick all seamen larn; And having got rid of a thumping quid,	*Hands by sides. Underline "larn". Say this line slowly as it is difficult to catch. After "quid" rapidly hawk and spit to your left. This gets a big laugh so wait for it.*
He spun this painful yarn:	*After "painful" wince, then say "yarn" immediately.*
" 'Twas in the good ship Nancy Bell, That we sailed to the Indian Sea;	*Don't forget old man's pose and accent. Right hand with spread palm indicates long voyage from left to right.*
And there on a reef, we come to grief— Which has often occurred to me.	*Agonized expression up to "grief". Very matter-of-fact delivery. Drop hands.*
And pretty nigh all the crew was drowned!	*"Drowned" should be very big and dramatic, with both hands raised and shaking à la Al Jolson singing "Mammy".*
There were seventy-seven o' soul;	*Signal the number seven backwards with both index fingers.*
But only ten of the Nancy's men, Said 'Ere!' to the muster roll.	*Indicate "ten" with fingers. On "Ere!" tug forelock with right hand. Drop for the rest of the line.*
There was me and the cook and the captain bold, And the mate o' the Nancy brig; And a bos'un tight, and a midshipmite, And the crew of the captain's gig.	*Movements as in third stanza. Speak mournfully but still briskly.*
For a month we'd neither wittles nor drink,	*On "wittles" mime biting into food held in left hand; on "drink" mime tilting a bottle with right hand.*
Till a-'ungry we did feel;	*Expression of pain on face and both hands flat on stomach.*
So we drawed a lot, an' accordin' —shot	*On "drawed" put left hand over eyes; on "lot" mime picking*

The captain for our meal!

The next lot fell to the Nancy's
   mate—
An' a delicate dish 'e made;

Then our appetite, with the
   midshipmite,
We seven survivors stayed.

Next we murdered the bos'un
   tight.

And 'e much resembled pig;

Then we wittled free, did the cook
   and me,

On the crew of the captain's gig.

Then only the cook and me was
   left,
And the delickit question—which
Of us two goes to the kettle,
   arose . . .
And we argued it out as sich.

Says 'e, 'Dear James, to murder
   me,

Were a foolish thing to do;
For don't you see, that you can't
   cook me,
While I can—and will—cook you!'

*name out of a hat with right hand.
On "accordin' " drop left hand, and
on "shot" mime firing gun with
right hand.
On "captain" assume pose as in
third stanza. Slight pause after
"captain".*

Mime telescope on "mate".

*Speak this line with surprised
delight; stress " 'e".*

*Naval salute and eyes uplifted on
"midshipmite".
Hands by sides.*

*Very grim expression—make the
most of "muuurdered". On
"bos'un" assume pose as in third
stanza.*

*Quite matter-of-fact, abruptly
breaking mood of previous line. On
"pig" briefly pick teeth with little
finger of left hand.*

*Resume grim manner. On "cook"
mime mixing as in third stanza; on
"me" point to yourself with right
thumb.*

As for third stanza. Very downbeat.

*Pick up tempo. Movements on
"cook and me" as in previous stanza.
On "which" raise right index finger.
On "us two" indicate him and
yourself with right hand.
On "argued" assume fighting stance.*

*On "Dear James" give big smile.
Very reasoning, almost patronizing
tones.
Stress foolish.
On "me" right hand on breast.*

*On "While I can" an evil glint in the
eye appears although the smile
should not be totally lost. "And will"
shows the threat becoming more
menacing; "cook you!"—the smile*

disappears and the right index finger points to stress the "you!".

So 'c boils the water an' takes the salt,

On "water" make circling motion with both hands to indicate large cooking-pot; on "salt" mime taking shaker in right hand.

And pepper in portions true;

On "pepper" take pot in left hand and shake.

And some chopped shallot, which 'e never forgot,

Chopping mime.

And some sage and parsley too!

Mime throwing sage in with right hand and parsley with left hand. Expression of extreme dismay.

Then 'e stirs it round and round and round,

Very slow and menacing, stirring the while.

And 'e sniffs at the boiling broth;

Give a sniff after "sniffs". Pause after broth, then unholy glint comes into the eye.

So I ups with 'is 'eels,

On "ups" mime lifting from floor level.

And I smothers 'is squeals,

On "smothers" mime holding lid down firmly with both hands. These two lines to be taken quickly.

In the scum of that foaming froth.

Pause. Sigh.

An' I eats that cook in a week or less,

And as I eating be, the last of 'is chops—

After "chops" mime chewing sickeningly on a bone—don't take too long on it.

Why—I almost drops!

Open eyes wide in surprise. On "drops" open fingers holding bone as though dropping it in satisfaction. Point out front on "wessel".

For a wessel in sight I see!

Drops hands. Pause.

And I never laugh, and I never smile,

Grim-faced. Measured tones.

And I never lark nor play.
But sit and croak a single joke,
I have, which is to say:

Upward inflection on "say".

Oh, I am a cook and a captain bold,

Very slow and dismal. Movements as for third stanza.

E*

And the mate of the Nancy brig;
And a bos'un tight, and a
  midshipmite,
And the crew of the captain's   *Encourage audience to join in last*
  gig."   *line.*

                                     Stand straight and drop head,
                                     keeping rhythm.

Notes: If "wittles" and "wessel" are thought not to suit the accent for the
wight, alter to victuals and vessel.

Keep all movements neat and controlled. Go cleanly from attitude to
attitude and when no specific pose is called for let your arms hang loosely
by your sides.

Observe the punctuation, and maintain the metre of every stanza strictly,
especially marking the internal rhyme in the third line of each.

Endeavour to differentiate the narrator when he is speaking to the audience
and when he is speaking to the wight.

OLD TIME CROSS-TALK ACT—ONE

C = Chairman or Straight Man   R = Red-nosed Comic

C: We would like to present for you now an act very rarely seen at this price range . . . in fact it's very rarely seen at all, and when it's over you'll understand why . . . no, we think there's still a lot of fun to be got out of this kind of act, and that's the old cross-talk comedy routine, you know—with the straight man and the red-nosed comedian. Now, we don't pretend that any of the jokes you are about to hear are in any way new . . . (*chuckle*) . . . should you recognize them, greet them as you would an old friend . . . with warmth and affection . . . laugh if you can, boo if you must, but don't just sit there—*do* something!

But first of all I'd like to give you the opening speech from Henry the Fifth by . . . er . . . by . . . special request.

"Oh, for a Muse of Fire! that would ascend——"

R: (*in audience*) Oi!

C: "—the brightest heaven of invention——"

R: (*approaching stage*) Oi! Do you know the way to the Town Hall?

C: Would you mind sitting down, sir? "—a kingdom for a stage——"

R: (*coming to his side*) Do you know the way to the Town Hall?

C: Would you go back to your seat, please, sir? "A kingdom for a stage——"

R: (*having gone away a pace or two and returned*) Do you know the way to the Town Hall?

C: (*angry*) No, I do not know the way to the Town Hall!   **169**

R: (*pointing*) Well, you go down the hill, and it's the second on the left! (*Runs round C to his other side*) 'Ere! I've just seen a man with a lemon stuck in his ear.

C: A man with a lemon stuck in his ear?

R: I went up to him I said, "What are you doing with that lemon stuck **170** in your ear?"

C: What did he say?

R: He said, "You've heard about the man with the hearing aid?"

C: Yes?

R: "Well, I'm the man with the lemon aid . . ."   **171**

C: Get off the stage! La, la, la, hmm, hmm, la, la . . .

R: (*going and returning*) What are you doing?

C: I'm just loosening up.

R: Sounds like you're falling apart. 'Ere—I shot my dog.   **172**

C: Was he mad?

173 R: He wasn't very pleased. I called him Fruit Salts.
     C: Why'd you call him Fruit Salts?
174 R: (*pointing to man in front row*) Ask him—'E knows . . . (Eno's.)
175 C: I think you're pusillanimous.
     R: No, I'm not, I'm C. of E. (*Sings*)
                  "Auntie Mary, had a canary,
176   Up the leg of her drawers——!"
     C: (*putting hand over his mouth*) That's enough of that!
     R: (*licking hand*) Mmm, Lifebuoy—my favourite.
177 C: What a terrible voice—you've got adenoids.
     R: Adenoids?
     C: Adenoids.
     R: Don't say that!
     C: Why not?
178 R: Adenoids me! (*That annoys me*) I've got seenus trouble, though.
179 C: Seenus trouble—you mean sinus.
     R: No, her husband came in and seen us. (*Runs round*) I'm taking her to
       the West Indies.
     C: Jamaica?
     R: No——
     R & C: Barbados!
180 C: Makes a change . . .
     R: 'Ere! Have a Garden of Eden cigar.
     C: What's a Garden of Eden cigar?
181 R: Once you've 'ad 'em you 'eave.
     C: Tell me, are there any more at home like you?
     R: Yes—there's my Mum and Dad.
     C: Your Mum and Dad?
182 R: They're in the Iron and Steel Trade. Mother irons and Father steals.
     C: All join in the chorus. . . . Are there any others?
     R: Yes, there's my brother.
     C: What does he do?
     R: He's a one-armed stonemason.
     C: How does he manage that?
183 R: He puts the chisel in his mouth and hits himself over the back of the
       head with a hammer.
     C: That's quite enough of this rubbish. If you won't let me recite perhaps
       you'll let me sing.
     R: What are you going to sing?
     C: Ladies and gentlemen, I'd like to give you—Clair de Lune.
     R: Clair de what?
     C: Clair de Lune.
184 R: I thought you said clear the room. (*To audience*) You haven't heard
       him sing. (*He does eccentric move and hurts himself, clutching on to*
       C) Oh, oh!
     C: What's the matter?
     R: I've twisted me truss.
     C: Truss you.

R: Thank you, Jock.
C: You've always got my support. 185
R: Can I sing with you?
C: All right, then, what would you like to sing?
R: I'd like to sing a little song, a little song entitled——
C: Yes?
R: Get out the meatballs, mother——
C: Yes?
R: We're coming to a fork in the road. 186
C & R: (*to pianist*) Thank you. (*Chord from piano*)
   Song: "The Miner's Dream of Home". C and R should illustrate each
   line of the song with an appropriate gesture. This should be done neatly
   and tidily, and during the gags the pose then arrived at should be held.)
C & R: (*singing*) "I saw the old homestead and faces I love,
                  I saw England's valleys and dells——"
R: My wife calls me dog. 187
C: Why?
R: Just a pet name.
C & R: (*singing*) "And I listened with joy,
                  As I did when a boy——"
C: She ought to call you budgerigar. 188
R: Why?
C: You always look so seedy.
C & R: (*singing*) "To the sound of the old village bells;
                  The fires were burning brightly,
                  'Twas a night that would banish all sin!—"
R: 'Ere, I didn't shave till was was twenty-four.
C: Where was your beard? 189
R: Down to my knees!
C & R: (*singing*) "For the bells were ringing the old year out——"
R: Do you know what the young girl said to the sailor? 190
C: No.
R: That's right!
C & R: (*singing*) "And the New Year in!"
   (*Piano plays in snappy 2/4 time for bows and R's exit*)
C: "Oh, for a Muse of Fire——"
R: (*running back on*) 'Ere! 'Ere! 'Ere!
C: What is it? What's the matter?
R: There's a fellow out there with a big bushy beard!
C: Is it a naval beard? 191
R: No, it grows on his chin! Oi! (*Jumps into C's arms*)
C: (*dropping him*) Get down, you fool. You must be drunk.
R: If I'm drunk, you're ugly. 192
C: You're drunk!
R: But in the morning I'll be sober . . . 'Ere, you're married, aren't you?
C: Yes I'm married.
R: He's got a lovely wife. I say—have you got any pictures of your wife
   in the nude?

193 C: No, I have *not*!

R: Wanna buy some . . .?

C: Ladies and gentlemen, I'd like to give you the perambulator song.

R: The perambulator song? How does that go?

194 C: It doesn't go—you push it! (*Pushes R*)

(*As C takes up singing pose R jumps to his side to join him*)

C & R: (*singing*) "I saw the old homestead and faces I love,
      I saw England's valleys and dells——"

R: Did you hear about the bull with a bad cold?

195 C: The bull with a bad cold? What happened?

R: The farmer bought him a Jersey.

C & R: (*singing*) "And I listened with joy,
       As I did when a boy,—"

R: Didn't do any good though. The bull died of pneumonia.

C: Why not?

196 R: The Jersey had a hole in it.

C & R: (*singing*) "To the sound of the old village bells
        The fires were burning brightly,
        'Twas a night that would banish all sin——"

R: I went out last night with a girl who stutters.

197 C: What happened?

R: By the time she said she wouldn't, she had!

C & R: (*singing*) "For the bells were ringing the old year out——"

R: Do you know what the young girl said to the sailor?

C: What again?

198 R: That's right!

C & R: (*singing*) "And the New Year——"

R: (*prodding C in stomach as he is about to take a big final note*) 'Ere!

C: What is it now?

R: I think they want to join in.

C: All right, then. Number —— on your song-sheets, this time with all the words and . . .

C & R: . . . with all the actions!

(*House lights come up. C & R wander to sides of stage encouraging the audience to do the actions*)

OMNES: "I saw the old homestead and faces I love,
     I saw England's valleys and dells;
     And I listened with joy,
     As I did when a boy,
     To the sound of the old village bells; (R: That's
      right, sir—pull it!)
     The fires were burning brightly,
     'Twas a night that would banish all sin;
     For the bells were ringing . . .
      (*C holds on to top note for a long time,
      eventually R gooses him and he squeaks*)
     The old year out——"

R: 'Ere!

C: What is it now?
R: Do you know what the young girl said to the sailor?   **199**
C: We've done that twice already.
R: That's right!
C & R: (*singing*) "And the Near Year in!"
   (*Piano plays fast 2/4 time. Bows and exits as after first chorus*)

Movements for "Miner's Dream of Home"

Both stand with feet at right-angles, left foot pointing straight at audience, with left hand holding coat lapel.

I saw the old homestead—	*Right hand flat over eyes.*
And faces I love,	*Right hand circles face twice; then both hands on heart.*
I saw England's valleys and dells;	*Right hand waves up and down.*
And I listened with joy,	*Right hand to ear.*
As I did when a boy,	*Right hand indicates small boy.*
To the sound of the old village bells.	*On the word "sound" both put hands together and mime bell-ringing—alternatively reaching up and bending at the knees for four bars.*
The fires were burning brightly;	*Both hands held out as though warming them at a fire. On "brightly" rub them together.*
'Twas a night—	*Right index finger raised.*
—that would banish all sin;	*Right hand makes sweeping motion.*
For the bells were ringing the old year out;	*As for bells above, but not bending at the knees.*
And the New Year in!	*More bell-ringing until last note, when the partners spread their arms out sideways.*

Note: With this act, it is important for the straight man not to become too aggressive with the comic. Although occasionally he might appear to become exasperated, he should always let it be seen that underneath he has an affection for this idiotic creature. This keeps the act happy and sunny-natured.

OLD TIME CROSS-TALK ACT—TWO

C = Chairman   R = Red-nosed Comic

C: Nostalgia time now, as we proudly present a recital of all those wonderful old jokes which have raised the Music Hall to its present state of near oblivion. But before then, I would like to give you in complete contrast, the famous soliloquy from *Hamlet* by er . . . er . . . William Shakespeare. Thank you. "To be, or not to be——"

R: (*entering*) 'Ere! I had dinner with him last night! I had dinner with Shakespeare.

C: You had dinner with Shakespeare? But he's been dead for three hundred and fifty years!

200 R: Blimey—I thought he was quiet. (*Turns to go then returns*) 'Ere's a funny thing—I call my dog Daisy.

C: Why do you call your dog Daisy?

201 R: Because some days 'e goes and some days 'e doesn't! I had to shoot him, though.

C: Why, was he mad?

R: No, just a bit eccentric.

202 C: I think you're pusillanimous.

R: No, I'm not—it's the way I walk. 'Ere—I took my wife to the East Indies.

C: Djarkata?

203 R: Yeah—in a wheelbarrow. My wife's got no nose.

C: How does she smell?

204 R: Terrible. I took my girl-friend to the West Indies.

C: Havana?

205 R: Now and then. (*Runs away and returns*) Doctor, Doctor—come quickly! My wife's just broken a leg!

C: But I'm a doctor of music!

206 R: That's all right—it's the piano leg! 'Ere—there's a one-legged man outside.

207 C: Tell him to hop it.

R: "I love the girls who do, I love the girls who don't;
I hate the girl who says she will,
And then she says she won't!
But the girl I love the best, and I'm sure you'll think I'm right,
Is the girl who says she never will—

208   But looks as though she might!"

C: Naughty! Naughty! What do you do for a living?

R: I'm a puppeteer.

C: A puppeteer! How did you get into that? 209
R: I had to pull a few strings. 'Ere—when I got married the vicar said, "Dost you take this woman?" I said, "I dost." IIe said, "Dost you take this man?" The wife said, "I dost." He said, "I now pronounce you a couple of dusters." 210
C: I don't think you're all there.
R: Oh yes I am. I saw my doctor only the other day. I said, "Doctor, my hair keeps falling out. Can you give me something to keep it in?"
C: Did he give you anything? 211
R: Yeah—a box. 'Ere—I call my girl-friend Yoyo.
C: Why? 212
R: I keep her dangling on a string. (*Calling*): "The train now standing at platform two, three, four and five has come in sideways!" 213
C: Are there any more at home like you?
R: There's my brother. He thinks he's a dog.
C: Thinks he's a dog?
R: Been like it since he was a puppy. 214
C: That's quite enough of this rubbish. Ladies and gentlemen, I'd like to sing for you now——
R: Can I join in?
C: If you must. What would you like to sing?
R: I'd like to sing a little song, a little song entitled:
C: Yes?
R: They call her Captain Kidd, 'cos she's got a sunken chest. 215
C & R.: (*to pianist*) Thank you.
(*Chord from piano for "Miner's Dream of Home". C & R should illustrate each line of the song with an appropriate gesture. This should be done neatly and tidily, and during the gags the pose then arrived at should be held.*)
C & R: (*singing*) "I saw the old homestead and faces I love,
　　　　　　　　I saw England's valleys and dells——"
R: Did you hear about the cannibal?
C: What about him? 216
R: IIe passed his brother in the jungle.
C & R: (*singing*) "And I listened with joy as I did when a boy——"
R: Every time I get drunk I see green hairy worms.
C: Have you see a doctor?
R: No, just green hairy worms. 217
C & R: (*singing*) "To the sound of the old village bells;
　　　　　　　　The fires were burning brightly,
　　　　　　　　'Twas a night that would banish all sin";
R: I went out with twins last night.
C: Did you have a good time? 218
R: Yes and no.
C & R: (*singing*) "For the bells were ringing the old year out——"
R: Do you know what the young girl said to the sailor?
C: No.
R: That's right!

C & R: (*singing*) "And the New Year in!"
    (*Music in fast 2/4 tempo as C and R take bows. R exits, returning almost immediately*)
  R: 'Ere! 'Ere! The invisible man's outside!
219 C: Tell him I can't see him!
  R: Wait a minute! Wait a minute! My brother keeps his wife under the bed.
  C: Why?
220 R: He thinks she's a little potty.
  C: I don't want to know about your family.
  R: Then there's my grandad—he's ninety-six.
  C: Ninety-six!
  R: He's got one foot in the grate.
221 C: You mean one foot in the grave . . .
  R: No, he wants to be cremated. 'Ere—I used to be a telegraph linesman.
  C: Why d'you give it up?
222 R: It drove me up the pole! (*Jumps into C's arms*)
  C: (*dropping him*) Get down, you fool. Ladies and gentlemen, I'd like to sing for you now——
  R: Oh, Mother!
223 C: I'll have you know my voice is trained.
  R: Trained? It's not even house-broken. *I'll* sing. I'd like to oblige now with the Song of the Pawnbroker.
  C: Song of the Pawnbroker?
224 R: "For You A-Loan".
  C & R: (*to pianist*) Thank you.
    (*Chord from piano. Gestures as before*)
  C & R: (*singing*) "I saw the old homestead and faces I love,
               I saw England's valleys and dells——"
  R: My girl-friend's got beautiful eyes, beautiful hair, beautiful teeth, etc., etc.
  C: Etcetera, etcetera?
225 R: Yeah—that's the best part of all.
  C & R: (*singing*) "And I listened with joy,
               As I did when a boy——"
  R: Did you hear about the nun with the wooden leg?
226 C: Who was she?
  R: Hopalong Chastity.
  C & R: (*singing*) "To the sound of the old village bells;
               The fires were burning brightly,
               'Twas a night that would banish all sin——"
  R: Did you hear about the nun on the penny-farthing?
  C: That's silly.
227 R: Silly? It's vergin' on the ridiculous!
  C & R: (*singing*) "For the bells were ringing the old year out——"
  R: Do you know what the sailor said to the young girl?
228 C: You've got it back to front.
  R: That's right!

C & R: (*singing*) "And the New Year——"
R: (*prodding C in the stomach as he prepares to take high note*) 'Ere!
C: What is it now?
R: I think they want to join in (*indicating audience*).
C: Very well, then. Number —— on your song-sheets; this time with all
    the words and——
C & R: —with all the actions!
    (*Chord from piano*)
    (*House lights come up. C & R wander to sides of stage and encourage
    the audience to participate in the actions*)
C & R: (*singing*) "I saw the old homestead and faces I love,
                I saw England's valleys and dells;
                And I listened with joy,
                As I did when a boy,
                To the sound of the old village bells:
                      R: That's right, sir—pull it!
                'The fires were burning brightly,
                'Twas a night that would banish all sin;
                For the bells were ringing the old year out . . ."
                (*C holds on to top note triumphantly,
                till R gooses him*)
                ". . . the old year out, a——"
                (*R digs C in the stomach*)
C: (*exasperated*) What is it now?
R: Do you know what the young girl said to the sailor?
C: This is getting ridiculous!   **229**
R: That's right!
C & R: (*singing*) "And the New Year in!"
    (*Music plays fast in 2/4 tempo for bows and R's exit*)

See page 67 for details of movements for "Miner's Dream".

TWELVE-MINUTE OLD TIME ACT

My own presentation of this act was as a Cockney but the patter is readily adaptable to any region. Nor is the song mandatory—I used *We All Come In the World With Nothing* because it is less hackneyed than many Music Hall songs, because I like the chorus melody, and because it suited the brash but earnest character I was seeking to portray. The lyrics are inoffensive, anonymous and non-comic so the interest and humour in the act derives solely from the patter and the manner of performance; if you choose to substitute another song while retaining the patter take care that the two remain compatible.

The following text is a transcript of a tape-recorded performance of this act at the Players' Theatre, Charing Cross, London. It was a particularly rowdy audience, containing a large and half-drunk party of dental students from London University. They had been dominating the audience and the show and by the time I came on—I was first after the second interval—they were well jugged up and loaded for beer. My fellow artistes had been coming off trembling and sweating; as the Chairman appeared to re-start the proceedings and to announce me, sounds of drunken badinage made him virtually inaudible, even in the wings. He banged his gavel, spoke my name—and into the lions' den I strode.

(As music plays introduction, picks up cigar (actually brought on in palm of hand) from stage. Sniffs it, grimaces, and with a slight indication of the head to the Chairman, says:)

230 Must be one of 'is . . . *(throws cigar away)* . . . nah then . . . Evening, Mr Chairman. Nice to see you . . . welcome home, may I say. Welcome back
231 . . . he's been abroad, you know . . . only tonight he's a feller . . . *(huge laugh and round of applause)* . . . no, shut up—I gotta get these trousers
232 back to the lodger . . . yes, he's been spending a bit of time in foreign parts, haven't you? . . . always very enjoyable, that is, yes . . . *(to Chairman)* blimey, you're right—they *are* slow! . . . 'Ere—hands up all those who've never been to the Players' Theatre before? . . . come on, be honest—hands up . . . bloody awful, in'it? . . . Now, ladies and gentlemen, as the Chairman told you, this is a beautiful song and it's going to be beautifully sung. *(To*
233 *pianist)* All right, Lil? Give us a quick archipelago and away we go.

Chord from piano. Leg shoots out and shakes. On first word jumps into pose, i.e. right heel tucked into arch of left foot and thumbs in belt. Takes the verse at breakneck speed—spoken, not sung—with the piano playing chords only.

Life is very funny when you come to think it out,
What a funny lot we are. Some——

Piano interrupts with two sharp loud chords. Does double-take at pianist.
Is that in it? (*Pianist: Yes!*) Strewth . . .
  Some of us are very rich and born without a doubt,
  Underneath a lucky star. You——

Piano interrupts with two chords, soft and harp-like this time.
Play that again.
*Chords are repeated, two octaves higher and even more dream-like, prompting
ecstatic expression. Voice from audience: "Beautiful!"*
  Quite right, mate. Wonderful musician, that girl . . . do you know, she's
been under some of the finest conductors in Europe . . .?   234
  You may be very poor but still it matters not,
  Never let it worry you what other folk have got;
  When a feller brags about the money that he's worth,
  Point it out (*picks up tune and slows down*) that all of us are equal
    on this earth,
  'Cos . . .

Incoherent shout from man in audience.
What was that, madam?

Man in audience: "Your trousers are too tight".
  They're not tight—I'm just pleased to see you. Now—that was the first
verseei, and here we come to the first choreei . . . I'd like you to pay particular attention if you will to the words and the toon, because when we
come to subsequent choreei we're gonna try a little experiment never before
attempted in this 'ere . . . 'All of Remembrance . . .

Another loud but incoherent male shout.
  Last time I saw a mouth like that there was a hook in it . . . (*laugh and
huge cheer*) . . . we're all against you, brother, so watch it! Now then——

Another interruption.
  Shut up! . . . that's what you call repartee . . . we're gonna ask you all to
join in with me—now there's a novelty for you. So what we're gonna do,
to encourage you, for the lady and gentleman what sing the best there will
be prizes, lovely prizes. For the lady what sings the best, she will have the
privilege of escorting me home after the performance—how about that
then, eh? . . . I'm staying over in Tooley Street at the moment, it's a lovely   235
spot at this time of year . . . where all the big nobs hang out . . . and for
the gentleman what sings the best——

Another interruption.
  Give us a chance! I been listening to you lot rabbitting on for two hours,
so give it a rest. I don't have to do this for a living, you know—I got two
chinchillas on heat . . .

Laugh out of which comes a male shout of "Get on with it".   236

I'll bet you say that to all the boys . . . as I was saying, the gentleman what sings the best, he will also get a wonderful prize—he will get a kiss, a kiss from Lil on the pianner . . . we take the candles off first so you'll be
237 all right . . . all right, sister, start pedalling.

Chord. During chorus, a steady well-marked 4/4 tempo, incorporate a simple dance where indicated.
> We all come in the world with nothing, No clothes to
> wear —(*dance*)
> When we die just bear in mind,
> All our troubles we must leave behind.
> Finish up just the same as we began,
> Without the slightest doubt,
> We all came in the world with nothing,
> And we can't take anything out!

How about that then, eh? Told you it was a beautiful thing, didn't I? Yes, ladies and gentlemen, that's the moral of the song—you can't take it with you . . . mind you, it's hard enough keeping hold if it while you're still
238 here, in'it? . . . The thing is, you gotta get a good job, you see. Now take me—I'm what they call a h'itinerant bespoke dustman . . . it's a good job —thirty bob a week and all I can eat . . . the only trouble is I have to do a lot of travelling. I was in a little seaside town the other week, a little seaside town. Stayed in a very nice hotel, just a stone's throw from the sea—you
239 couldn't miss it, all the windows were broken.

Anyway, on the Sunday when I arrived I banged on the door. The landlady answered—quite fair she was. You know, forty and fruity. She said "yes?" I said, "Wait a minute—I haven't asked you yet!" She said, "What
240 do you want?" I said, "I wanna stop here for the week." She said, "Do
241 you want food?" I said, "Why, is there anything else?" She said, "Well, anyway, I can't take you—we're all full up." I said, "Oh, you can squeeze
242 me in a back room somewhere, can't you?" She said, "I could, but I haven't got the time!" I said she was fruity . . . she said, "You can sleep with baby." I said, "Sleep with baby! Nah . . . none of that—I can walk about
243 and get wet through." So she said, "Well, you can sleep on the couch." I said, "That'll do me fine, love. How much?" She said, "Fifteen bob a
244 week all in . . . and I don't want any children . . ."

Blimey, I thought you were gonna miss that for a minute . . .

So I said, "All right, love, that'll do." And I slept on the couch. Six o'clock in the morning, in walks this beautiful blonde . . . wearing nothing . . . but a negleej . . . and carrying a cup of tea! I said to her, "Who are you?" She said, "I'm Baby. Who are you?" I said, "I'm the mug that
245 slept on the couch . . .!"

Anyway, I went home that week-end—there's a funny thing: I went home!—the train was late and I didn't get in till four in the morning. The wife was going up the wall! She said, "Where've you been?" I said, "I couldn't help it—the train was late." She said, "You should have been here. We've had a burglar." I said, "Blimey—did he get anything?" She
246 said, "Yes—I thought it was you!"

(*Laughs and groans*)
 I know how you feel . . . (*indicating party of students*) . . . I'm not wasting
my best gags on that lot . . . (*To pianist, a very dark girl*) You ready,
Ginge? Here we go, then. Second verse.
 My advice to those who want to lead a happy life,
 Whether you be rich or poor,
 Is laugh away your troubles!
(*Gives loud cackle. Audience falls silent, expecting a gag*) That's shut 'em
up for the first time tonight!
 You must never think of strife,
 Think of better days in store.
 Life——
(*To pianist*) I'm beating her tonight!
 Life can be a pleasure if you go the proper way,
 Do not worry over little items every day;
 Keep it in your memory that life is but a span,
 While we're here (*slows down and picks up tune*)
  let's make our lives worth living if we can!
 'Cos——(*Speaks to wings*) House lights!
 We all came—— (*No house lights*) House lights! Oi, Ada . . .
 (*Walks to wings*) Give us a bit of glim, gal . . . Ada, what are you
 doing——? (*walks back down centre with look of disgust*) she's
 sandpapering her bunions . . . (*Looks off again*) Lights please,
 love . . . (*Lights come on*)
 Now then, let's have a look at you . . . (*grimaces*) . . . that was a mistake 247
 . . . evening, dear . . . no, don't pick your nose, love . . . that's a nice turn
 of leg you got there, missus . . . pity it's only the one . . .   248
 Now then—all got your race-cards? As the Chairman told you this one's
 number X for those of you that can read . . . no, I didn't think you lot
 could . . . they're printed in English so if you happen to be a foreigner this
 might be a good time to go and water the horses . . . any foreigners in,
 Mr Chairman? (*Chairman: "A few"*) A few? Ah well, then, for the
 foreigners: main-ten-ong . . . vou . . . poovay—you know what poovay
 means, don't you? . . . yes, I thought *you* would . . . you poovay allay . . .
 er . . . descendez . . . apples and pears-ay . . . er . . . à la pissoir . . . (*Turns
 to Chairman during laugh and says:*) That's not bad, is it?   249
 I speak it like a native, you know . . . not much like a Frog but just like
 a native . . . I picked it up at London University . . . (*big reaction from
 dental students*) . . . that's not the only thing I picked up there, neither . . .
 never mind . . . all got your song-sheets? Wave 'em at me . . . that's nice,
 it gets a bit stuffy in here . . . all right, don't all go raving mad . . . I'll get
 through this turn if it kills me . . . come on, now—Lil wants to get home 250
 before the pills wear off . . .
 As you've heard this is a beautiful thing so perhaps you'd like to open up
 the tubes a bit before we start . . . (*Coughs and audience does likewise,
 disgustingly*) Oh, very genteel, I'm sure . . .

Loud solo belch from audience.

Thank you, Mother . . . shall we have a little tune-up? Give us a B flat,
251 Lil—no, give us a B. We'll flatten it ourselves.

*Piano plays note. Audience sing it. One loud and very high tenor carries on
long after.*
    I'm glad I don't have to do your laundry . . . (*screams of mirth and
cheers*) . . . too easy, too easy . . . (*laugh goes on and on. As it dies down one
woman is still laughing helplessly*) . . . you having a spasm there, love? . . .
put your head between your knees . . . take the fag out first, though . . .
252 don't want to spoil your week-end . . . come on, let's have a proper tune-up.

Piano plays note. Audience sings it.
    La—la—laaaa! . . . Blimey, from here it looks like a dentist's nightmare!
(*Laughs and cheers*) Did I tell you my wife hates going to the dentist?
Hates it, she does . . . looking at you lot, I'm not surprised . . . now then
. . . last time she had to go for a filling she said to the dentist, "I'm so
nervous. I hate coming here. I don't know which is worse—having a
filling or having a baby." He said, "Well, make up your mind before I
adjust the chair . . . !" . . . no, don't applaud, don't applaud, it's not worth
it . . . every one a classic . . . All right, Lil, start pedalling: (*Chord*)
        We all come in the world with nothing, no clothes to wear;
        When we die just bear in mind,
        All our troubles we must leave behind.
        Finish up just the same as we began,
        Without the slightest doubt;
        We all came in the world with nothing,
        And we can't take anything out!

One bar bridge taking the key up a tone.
(*Spoken*) Last chance tonight! We—
—all come in the world with nothing, no clothes to wear;
        When we die just bear in mind,
        All our troubles we must leave behind;
        Finish up just the same as we began,
        Without the slightest doubt;
        We all came in the world with nothing,
        And we can't take anything out!
Thank you very much, ladies and gentlemen, good night and God Bless—
I'm glad to get off in one piece—and always remember, all of you:
        (*Spoken*) We all came in the world with nothing . . .
        (*Sung andante*) And we can't take anything . . . out!

Piano plays last eight bars presto and fortissimo for calls.

253 *Note: Instead of "that's shut 'em up for the first time tonight!" (second
verse) you can say "hasn't it gone quiet—must be a lousy act on . . ." Or
"what are you all staring at . . .?" Or (yawn) "I'm ready for bed—anyone . . .?"*

INDEX

The numbers refer to the jokes and not to the pages